Albertanus of Brescia

Nec hoc promitto in uno tempore· nihil in me super esse quod mutandum sit.
quid ni multa habeam que debeant colligi. quae extenuari· quae attolli·
Et hoc ipsum argumentum est· in melius translati animi· quod uitia sua que
adhuc ignorabat uideo· quibusdam egris gratulatio fit· cum ipsos
aegros se esse senserunt· Cuperem itaq; tecum communicare· tam subi
tam mutationem mei· Tunc amicitiae nostrae certiorem fiduciam
habere cepissem· Illius uere quam non spes· non timor· non utilita
tis sue cura diuellit· Illius cum qua homines moriuntur· pro qua mori
untur· multi· Multi tibi dabo qui non amico sed amicitia caruerint· hoc
non potest accidere cum amicos· in societatem honesta cupiendi par uolun
tas trahit· Quid ni possit· Sciunt enim ipsos omnia habere commu
nia· Et quidem magis· aduersa concipere animo non potest· quantum
momenti afferre mihi singulos dies uideam· Mitte inquis et nobis ista
quae tam efficacia expertus es· Ego uero omnia in te cupio transfun
dere· et in hoc aliquid gaudeo discere· ut doceam· Nec me ulla res
delectabit lic et sit eximia et salutaris· quam mihi uni sciturus sum·
Si cum hac exceptione detur sapientia ut illam inclusam teneam nec
enuntiem· reiciam· Nullius boni sine socio iocunda possessio est·
Mittam itaq; ipsos tibi libros· et ne multum opere impendas dum
passim profutura sectaris· Inponam notas ut ad ipsa protinus
que probo et miror accedas· Plus te tamen uiua uox et uita
quam oratio proderit· In re presente· m uenias oportet· Primum
quia homines amplius oculis quam auribus credunt· deinde
quia longum iter est per precepta· breue et efficax per exempla·
Zenonem cleanter non expressisset· Si tantummodo audisset·
uite eius inter fuit· Secreta perspexit· et obseruauit illum an for
mula sua uiueret· Platon et aristotiles et omnis in diuersum
itura sapientium turba· plus ex moribus quam ex uerbis so
cratis traxit· Metrodorum et hermarchum et polienum
magnos uiros non scola epicuri· sed contubernium magnum fecit·

Albertanus of Brescia

The Pursuit of Happiness in the Early Thirteenth Century

James M. Powell

μ𝑝𝑝

University of Pennsylvania Press
Philadelphia

BX
4705
.A447
P68
1992

University of Pennsylvania Press
MIDDLE AGES SERIES
Edited by Edward Peters
Henry Charles Lea Professor
of Medieval History
University of Pennsylvania

A complete listing of the books in this series
appears at the back of this volume

Publication of this book has been aided by the Vice-President for
Research, Syracuse University.

Frontispiece: MS Brescia Queriniana. B.II.6, f.4v. (tenth century). Seneca, *Epistolae morales
ad Lucilium*. Reproduced with the authorization of the Director of the Biblioteca Civica
Queriniana of Brescia, as by the protocol 254/10 April 1991.

Library of Congress Cataloging-in-Publication Data
Powell, James M.
    Albertanus of Brescia : the pursuit of happiness in the early thirteenth century / James M.
Powell.
        p.   cm. — (Middle Ages series)
    Includes bibliographical references and index.
    ISBN 0-8122-3138-4
    1. Albertanus, of Brescia, 13th cent.   I. Title.   II. Series.
    BX4705.A447P68   1992
    945'.2604'092—dc20
                                                                          91-29777
                                                                              CIP

For
Jeremy, Jason,
Stephanie Ann, and Jennette

Contents

Acknowledgments

DURING THE ACADEMIC YEAR 1989–90, I was privileged to be a visiting member at the Institute for Advanced Study. I wish to thank the Institute, its faculty, especially Giles Constable, and my fellow visiting members for their support and advice during the writing of this book. I would also like to thank Syracuse University, the Maxwell School, Dean John Palmer, and my colleagues for the leave that enabled me to accept this opportunity. I owe a special "thank you" to the staffs of the Institute's School of Historical Studies and its library. Its medieval seminar was also very valuable for me. Grants from the American Philosophical Society and the Senate Research Committee provided support to study in numerous European libraries. I would like to thank the staffs of these libraries for their kindness and assistance. If I single out merely a few for mention, it is not because I value the others less, but because the efforts of those mentioned here were more particularly helpful. Leonard Boyle, Prefect of the Vatican Library, and Rosa Zilioli Faden of the Biblioteca Queriniana in Brescia provided unique assistance in securing material. The staffs of the archives in Venice, Brescia, and Milan were very helpful in enabling me to search for documents relevant to this study. Despite the fact that the Biblioteca Riccardiana was closed, I was received and assisted most graciously. I must also thank Dr. D. S. H. Abulafia for extending the hospitality of Gonville and Caius College and the librarians for opening their excellent manuscript collection to me. I would also like to thank the staffs of Cambridge University Library, the British Library, the Lambeth Library, the Guild Hall Library, the University of Pavia Library, the Bibliothèque Nationale, the Ambrosiana, the Biblioteca Nazionale in Florence, the Marciana, and the Biblioteca Nacionál in Madrid. Closer to home, I wish to thank John Henneman for a fine introduction to the Firestone Library, where I spent many evenings. Dorcas MacDonald and the Interlibrary Loan staff at Bird Library were their usual helpful selves, as were their colleagues in other departments of the library.

A list of all the individuals who helped in this project would be difficult to make. Jim Muldoon read and commented on a chapter of the manuscript. He was a great sounding board. I am grateful to Professor Edward M. Peters, to the editorial staff of the University of Pennsylvania Press, and to the very helpful readers of the manuscript. I thank Alan Bernstein for the reference to Hedwige Peemens-Poullet's thesis. Father Masetti-Zanini, director of the Episcopal Archives in Brescia, gave me a crash course in local history along with access to his beautifully organized archive. My colleague Ken Pennington and my good friend Jim John advised me on matters of paleography. Jane Frost typed the manuscript. Finally, I wish to express my warmest gratitude to my wife and family. Their support and interest has meant so much to me that no words can express it.

Abbreviations

H.-B.	Huillard-Bréholles, Jean L. A. *Historia diplomatica Friderici Secundi*. 6 vols. Paris, 1852–61.
LP	*Liber potheris communis civitatis Brixiae*. In *Historiae patriae Monumenta*, vol. 19. Turin, 1899.
Loeb ed.	Loeb Classical Library.
Meersseman, *Dossier*	Meersseman, Gérard G., *Dossier de l'ordre de pénitence*. Paris, 1982.
MGH Ep.	*Monumenta Germaniae Historica. Epistolae Saeculi XIII*. 3 vols. Edited by Carl Rodenburg. Munich, 1982.
MGHSS	*Monumenta Germaniae Historica. Scriptores*.
Moralium	*Das moralium philosophorum de Guillaume de Conches*. Edited by John Holmberg. Uppsala, 1929.
Muratori, *Antiquitates*	Muratori, Lodovico. *Antiquitates Italicae medii aevi*. 6 vols. Milan, 1738–42.
Ordo fraternitatis	Meersseman, Gérard G., *Ordo fraternitatis: Confraternite e pietà dei laici nel medioevo*. 3 vols. Rome, 1977.
PL	*Patralogia Latina*. Edited by J. P. Migne. Paris, 1844–65.
Pressutti	*Regesta Honorii Papae III*. 2 vols. Edited by Petrus Pressutti. 1888. Reprint. Hildesheim, 1978.
RISS	*Rerum Italicarum scriptores*. 28 vols. Edited by L. A. Muratori. Milan, 1723–51.
RISS, n.s.	*Rerum Italicarum scriptores*. New series. Edited by G. Carducci et al. Città di Castello, 1900–.

RS   *Rolls Series: The Chronicles and Memorials of*
                            Great Britain and Ireland During the Middle
                            Ages. London, 1858–.
Sermones quattuor   *Sermones quattuor: Edizione curata sui codici*
                            bresciani. Edited by Marta Ferrari. Lonato,
                            1955.
Storia di Brescia   *La storia di Brescia.* 4 vols. Edited by Giovanni
                            Treccani degli Alfieri. Brescia, 1963.

Introduction

In August 1238, the forces of Emperor Frederick II laid siege to Brescia. Their aim was to punish the Brescians, who had joined the Milanese in the revived Lombard League and had prevented Frederick from reestablishing imperial rule in Italy. Brescia, though not strategically as important as Milan, controlled the western shore of Lake Garda and the route to Riva and the Trentino. Like almost all of the cities of the region, Brescia was politically divided. Some leading citizens and nobles of the city and surrounding countryside supported the emperor; others, perhaps most, felt that the interests of Brescia lay with Milan and the Lombard League. As part of their plan of defense, the Brescians had placed Albertanus, from the quarter of Santa Agata on the western edge of the city, in command of the fortress of Gavardo, which protected the route from Salò on Lake Garda. Gavardo was hardly secure. The inhabitants had a record of disloyalty. Not surprisingly, the fort fell to Frederick and Albertanus was taken prisoner. We do not know anything about the circumstances or terms of surrender, but Albertanus was turned over to Frederick's allies, the Cremonese, and imprisoned in their city. Though his stay in prison was apparently fairly short, it marked the beginning of a writing career for this rather obscure Brescian judge and *causidicus*.[1]

During the next twelve years or so, Albertanus produced three treatises and five sermons, the latter addressed to fellow members of professional confraternities in Genoa and Brescia. His first treatise, written while he was imprisoned and entitled *De amore et dilectione Dei et proximi et aliarum rerum et de forma vitae*, was addressed to his son Vincentius. While in Genoa in 1243 as assessor to his fellow Brescian Emmanuel de Madiis (Maggi), podestà of Genoa, he addressed a sermon to his Genoese colleagues. In 1245, after his return from Genoa, he wrote the *De doctrina dicendi et tacendi* for his son Stephanus. The *Liber consolationis et consilii*, which takes the form of a dialogue between Melibeus and his wife Prudence on the risks involved in the private vendetta, was written for his son Joannes, a surgeon, in 1246. Finally, around 1250, he wrote four sermons, which he delivered to his fellow *causidici* in Brescia.[2] This body of writing represents a large and mostly untapped resource not merely for the study of an early thirteenth-century layman, but also for better understanding his society.

Although previous writers have stressed the paucity of documents available for a study of Albertanus, he is surprisingly well-documented for a person of his station. True enough, there is no contemporary mention in chronicles; nor are there letters that provide intimate details of his personal and family life, but such things are rare even for the best-known medieval figures. There is, however, ample information to study his career and his place in the social and political life of Brescia. The circumstances of his professional life are illustrated by documents from every period. From this evidence, a concrete picture of this Brescian professional man and a context for his writing and thinking begin to emerge.

The earliest mention of Albertanus is in a renewal of the Lombard League undertaken at Brescia on 7 April 1226, in which he appears as Albertanus *judex* immediately after another Brescian judge, Petrus Villanus.[3] We know nothing securely about his education or his early years. At the time of his appearance, he was undoubtedly a young man. Although Aldo Checchini and others have speculated about his education, especially regarding his possible legal study at Bologna or Padua, there is no definite evidence of this and the research presented later suggests otherwise.[4] His family background is obscure. He never used a patronymic, as was becoming customary at this time. Instead, he identified himself by the section of the city in which he lived, as Albertanus "de oria Sancte Agate."[5] In 1250, in a sermon delivered in the Franciscan church of San Giorgio Martire, Albertanus mentions that he had then been in practice of his profession for almost twenty-five years, thus suggesting that his appearance as a witness to the oath of the rectors of the second Lombard League was one of his earliest professional acts.[6] This treaty, when taken in conjunction with other documents, places him among the members of the anti-imperial group that was emerging in Brescia in the 1220s for reasons indicated in the next chapter. His identification with the interests of the commune is suggested by his participation in the purchase of lands for the *Broletto*, or city hall, in 1227.[7] During the 1230s, he was actively involved in the *inquisitiones* conducted by the commune in pursuit of its rights and properties in various parts of the *contado*.[8] His role as a counselor in these matters was firmly established, as the records make clear. Since these were issues that often led to conflict, he must be judged an expert in both legal and practical matters during this period.

Two major events stand out in his adult life. The first was his captaincy of the fortress of Gavardo in 1238 and his ensuing captivity in Cremona.[9] There can be no question that this represented a turning point in his life. It was this experience that led to the writing of his first treatise, although he must already have studied and read considerably. His involvement in active life up to that time, however, would not have been conducive to writing. His term as a prisoner provided both motive and opportunity. Moreover, his son Vincentius was still rather young in 1238. Even if Albertanus had married before beginning his career in 1226, it is probable that Vincentius would have been no more than eighteen. Recent experience may also have convinced Albertanus of the wisdom of writing some advice to his son. But we ought not to confuse Albertanus's intentions with those of the later writers of *memorie,* who celebrated family deeds and offered personal advice to their sons. His purpose was at once more didactic and more broadly conceived.

The second event to single out was his position as legal counselor of his fellow countryman Emmanuel de Madiis (Maggi), podestà of Genoa in 1243.[10] By this time, Albertanus enjoyed a considerable reputation in professional circles, as we learn from the fact that he delivered a sermon before a confraternity of Genoese judges and notaries meeting in the house of Petrus de Nigro. He was closely identified with the Maggi, one of the leading families in Brescia, whose star continued to rise throughout the thirteenth century, especially with the election of Emmanuel's son, Berardus, as bishop of Brescia and de facto ruler of the city in the 1270s.[11] Emmanuel himself served as podestà of Parma in 1251, but Albertanus was then involved in the diplomatic affairs of the commune and did not accompany him there or to Rome, where Emmanuel served as senator until his death in 1256.[12] By that time, Albertanus had probably died, for the last document to record his presence, a treaty of peace with Bergamo, is dated 11 May 1251.[13] There is a certain fitting quality in the life of this man who wrote so much about peace and whose last public act was to participate as a witness in a treaty of peace.

The documents relating to Albertanus show that he succeeded in creating a niche for himself within the structure of the Brescian ruling classes. Allied to a group of important civic leaders, he maintained a professional stance that secured him against the extremes of partisanship. He was a mediator not merely by profession but probably also by temperament. To understand his writings, we must recognize that he was always conscious of his actual status and role in Brescian society. Without talking about himself, he provided considerable evidence about what it meant to live as a member of the professional class in the insecurity of a violent society. His writings are the product of a man deeply concerned about the problems of his society, fully conscious of the inadequacies of the means available to ensure justice, but committed to finding better ways to improve conditions of life. Above all, he was a man of the commune.

The present study focuses on his writings. But it begins with the premise that they can be understood only within the context of the community in which he lived and wrote. For this reason, this volume examines major features of life in Brescia in the early thirteenth century, particularly as they affected Albertanus and those with whom he came into contact. Certain aspects of communal life seem to have a special impact on the writings of Albertanus. The violence of medieval society inspired much of what he wrote. Likewise, his attitude toward heresy owed much to the situation in Brescia. The approaches that he took to understand the nature of his society and to attempt to create a theoretical framework of social organizations, however, proved to be extraordinarily original. This study of Albertanus's works provides an opportunity to view a medieval mind at work in a way not often possible. Through his works, we can gain additional insight into the creativity of medieval thought. Most particularly, we can see how some of the major developments of twelfth-century thought began to find expression in the mind of an early thirteenth-century thinker. The emergence in the twelfth century of a new moral science in such works as the *Moralium dogma philosophorum*, attributed to William of Conches, and in the *summas* produced in the circle around Peter the Chanter in Paris at the turn of the century points to a significant change in the mode of analysis of human behavior.[14] At the same time, the widespread experimentation with forms of social and political organization in this period suggests an openness to fundamental structural changes that seems at variance with the conservative views often expressed in contemporary sources regarding the nature of the social order. Finally, Albertanus's stress on the role of urban professionals transcends the approaches taken by many of his contemporaries.

The argument here is not that Albertanus set forth a body of new social theory that dramatically affected the direction of social and political thought in the next two hundred years. Even though there might be some merit to such an argument, it appears to me to venture into a realm already overpopulated by extravagant claims. Rather, the focus of this book is on his largely unrecognized contribution as an original thinker, and the way in which it developed from a confrontation between life experience and learning experience. How did these two forms of experience combine in the late twelfth and early thirteenth centuries to produce new ideas about society and human relationships? Albertanus certainly made extensive use of earlier authorities. He was especially indebted to Seneca and to the Wisdom literature of the Old Testament. How did he use this material?[15] If we are to regard him as original, in what did that originality consist? In Albertanus, we can study the manner in which learning and experience combined to form a new synthesis. This study argues that the creativity of medieval thought cannot be understood solely through a study of classical and biblical sources or the combing of *florilegia, exempla,* or the writings of other medieval authors. The example of Albertanus suggests a much more complex picture of medieval approaches to social theory than that previously studied in the literature.

Interest in Albertanus has largely been confined to students of medieval literature, for it is among later medieval and Renaissance authors that his influence has been most apparent. Already in the second half of the thirteenth century, his works began to appear in translation. Andrea da Grosseto translated his three treatises from Latin into Tuscan in 1268 and 1269. Within a short time, other translations into Italian appeared, to be followed by those into other languages.[16] Brunetto Latini, occupied in preparing his *Livres dou Tresor* in Paris during the second half of the century, made extensive use of Albertanus's *De doctrina dicendi et tacendi,* which had been written as recently as 1245.[17] While Dante nowhere makes a direct reference to Albertanus, Santino Caramella and others have found traces of his works in the writings of the poet.[18] In England, John Gower certainly knew the writings of Albertanus, but the most famous example is that of Geoffrey Chaucer, who adapted his "Tale of Melibee" from a French version of Albertanus's *Liber consolationis et consilii.*[19] In the fifteenth century, the *Ménagier de Paris* upheld Prudence, the wife of Melibeus, as an ideal woman for those who would read his manual of instruction for young wives.[20] Likewise, traces of Albertanus's influence appeared in the Italian *Fiore di virtù.*[21] Other examples will be discussed more thoroughly in the final chapter of this volume, which is devoted to the way Albertanus's writings were utilized during the later Middle Ages.

Aside from these examples, however, it is worth noting here that hundreds of manuscripts of Albertanus's writings in Latin and various vernaculars, written between the thirteenth and the sixteenth centuries, are found widely scattered in European libraries.[22] Toward the end of this period, various printed editions appeared, most notably that prepared at Cuneo in 1507.[23] Thereafter, particularly in the later sixteenth and seventeenth centuries, the reputation of Albertanus declined, save among local writers in Brescia.

Only in the nineteenth century, due largely to studies of the sources of Chaucer and other medieval writers, was there a growing awareness of the significance of Albertanus's works. Thor Sundby published editions of the *Liber consolationis et consilii* in 1873 and the *De doctrina dicendi et tacendi* in 1884. He made a conscientious effort to prepare critical editions, but was hampered by the unavailability of some of the more important manuscripts, especially those in the Vatican Library. Despite their defects, however, his editions played an important role in the revival of studies on Albertanus of Brescia in the late nineteenth century. At the same time, Monsignor Luigi Fè d'Ostiani, who worked tirelessly to promote interest in the history of his native Brescia, edited Albertanus's sermon to the *causidici* and notaries of Genoa in 1243. Fè d'Ostiani's edition, published in 1874, was not easily available beyond Brescia, however, and had little influence outside of Italy. He did have access to a number of good manuscripts, however, and, while his edition cannot be considered definitive, it remains most useful. It is not surprising, given these limitations, that no book-length study of Albertanus has appeared to date.[24]

Although relatively little attention has been given to the content of Albertanus's works, there has been a near-constant stream of essays dealing with the man himself, his education, his relationship to the intellectual movements of the thirteenth and fourteenth centuries, and his influence on other writers and their use of his works. As an exception to these studies, Gérard Meersseman's essays on Albertanus as a lay preacher and on confraternities in Brescia explore a dimension first opened by Fè d'Ostiani and expanded by the publication of Marta Ferrari's edition of four sermons delivered by Albertanus in the Franciscan house at San Giorgio Martire in Brescia about 1250.[25] Ferrari's edition, though based on only two manuscripts, calls attention to the importance of this aspect of Albertanus's activity. Despite considerable interest in the history of confraternities, particularly in Italy, there has been no recent effort to follow up the initiative undertaken by Meersseman.

As we have already noted, little is known about Albertanus. Research for the present book has yielded only a single additional document dealing with his professional activity. The most important early research has focused on his education. As we have already seen, Aldo Checchini presented the basic evidence concerning Albertanus's legal education. Through an examination of legal citations and rhetorical usages, he attempted to show that Albertanus studied at the University of Bologna.[26] This view has been widely adopted, including in its adherents Marta Ferrari, who has written an extensive article on the sermons of Albertanus in which she has reexamined earlier literature on Albertanus's life and education.[27] However, Checchini was not able to provide decisive evidence in support of his view.

An even more difficult question has been the place of Albertanus in the writings of the twelfth and thirteenth centuries. Francesco Novati was among the earliest to group him with the so-called pre-humanists, a group of writers, chiefly Paduan and Florentine, notable for their legal training and their interest in the classics and in the writing of history.[28] But more recent scholarship in the field has tended to ignore Albertanus. Not only is he not mentioned in important studies by Roberto Weiss and Giuseppe Billanovich, but he has no place in the recent essays published in Albert Rabil's collection on humanism.[29] In part, this may be explained by the clear ties between Albertanus and the twelfth-century Senecans, as presented by Leighton Reynolds in *The Medieval Tradition of Seneca's Letters* and by Claudia Villa in her important article on the Brescian manuscript of Seneca's letters to Lucilius and its use by Albertanus, which follows a suggestion made by Reynolds in his work.[30] No one familiar with the writings of Albertanus is likely to link them to the Paduans, and only indirect connections appear to exist with later humanistic writings.[31] Some of these will receive attention in the present book. Here I would only suggest that the common interest in ethics shared by Albertanus and the humanists is worthy of further exploration.

Aside from a continuing local interest that has produced numerous studies of Albertanus, the most consistent body of writing concerns his use by later writers. For the most part, these authors have little interest in Albertanus; their attention is on bigger fish. Maria Corti has studied "Le fonti del *Fiore di Virtù* e la teoria della 'Nobiltà' nel duecento," which sheds light on Albertanus's influence on this genre. Conrad Mainzer has discussed Albertanus's influence on John Gower's *Confessio amantis*. Recent discussions of Chaucer and the "Tale of Melibee" are found in Charles Owen's article published in 1973 and Paul Olson's *The Canterbury Tales and the Good Society* (1986). As early as 1944, Gardner Stillwell attempted to pursue the question of the political meaning of the "Tale of Melibee," thus recognizing the evident thrust of this treatise. But Chaucer scholars have made little effort to compare his version of the "Tale of Melibee" with that of Albertanus in order to study the differences between them.[32]

This book, though indebted to this earlier literature, takes a different tack. It studies Albertanus within the context of the effort of north Italian communes in the thirteenth century to establish order and peace within a particular region and against the factional background endemic to communal society. Albertanus was conscious of the fragility of the ties that bound his society together and of the threat posed by the powerful to the poor and powerless. Throughout his writings, the notion of liberation of the poor crops up again and again.[33] It is important to keep in mind that he wrote primarily for those who shared his own experience. He addressed his sons and his fellow *causidici*. He was not only the product of an Italian commune, but of a particular commune. He was an urban professional and was particularly concerned with the role of such professionals in society. In the chapters that follow, the question of Albertanus's urban background and professional education forms an underlying theme in the effort to understand his writings.

To some degree, his writings are surprising not only for what they contain, but for what they do not contain. For example, we would certainly expect that Albertanus would be concerned about usury. It was a major topic for most of the writers of the period who dealt with the problems of the cities. In particular, given his relations with the Franciscans and perhaps also the Dominicans, a concern about the impact of interest charges on the poor would be natural. But Albertanus, though he condemned usury, had no great interest in this topic as such.[34] This fact is all the more strange in that he devotes considerable space to the needs of the poor and to freeing the poor from the dominance of the rich and powerful. This example suggests the considerable risk in generalizing about the attitudes of members of the educated laity like Albertanus. One of the values of this study lies in its effort to expose the tensions that underlay early thirteenth-century communal society. For in spite of the considerable progress that has been made in this field in recent decades, there is still a tendency to view these tensions more in terms of the papal/imperial dichotomy summed up by the names Guelph and Ghibelline than in terms of the political and social evolution of communal societies.

Earlier historians tended to see the guiding hand of political ideology and international diplomacy as major factors in shaping political factions in thirteenth-century communes. This view has been revised in recent scholarship but continues to exercise some influence. The approach taken here stresses the importance of local factions, which were largely the product of the same tensions that brought about the creation of the commune and which were evident in the conflicts of institutions and of powerful individuals and groups. Only later, as broader issues emerge, do these factions tend to coalesce behind the leaders of imperial and papal factions or parties.

There can be no doubt about Albertanus's loyalty to the commune and, most especially, to the Brescian commune, which identified its interests with those of the papacy and the Lombard League, though not necessarily in that order. But the situation at the beginning of the thirteenth century was markedly different from that which developed in the 1240s and later. Albertanus and his contemporaries did not face the papal/imperial dichotomy to the same degree as the next generations. The issues that seemed so clear-cut to an early fourteenth-century political theorist like Marsilius of Padua, and that marked the *Defender of the Peace* as an anti-papal polemic, were scarcely articulated before the 1240s and 1250s. They find no place in the writings of Albertanus. But this does not mean that the attitudes that gave rise to these conflicts and the issues that fed them are entirely absent, merely that there was a different spirit in the early part of the century, especially the 1220s and 1230s, one that was imbued with the positive possibilities for the reform of church and society.

Whether we focus on the Fourth Lateran Council, with its extensive program for reform of the church, or on the growing emphasis on the study of law in such centers as Bologna and Padua, it is relatively easy to catch glimpses of these concerns. But the most apparent evidence of the spirit of reform is undoubtedly to be found in the religious movements, clerical and lay, that sprang up through much of Europe in the eleventh and twelfth centuries. The return to the primitive ideals of monasticism, the imitation of Christ and his apostles in the apostolic life, the rejection of wealth and the embrace of voluntary poverty, all signaled the birth of a new spirit that affected clergy and laity alike.

Brescia was no stranger to reform. The memory of Arnold of Brescia, whose radical critique of both church and secular society had rocked twelfth-century Rome, must still have been fresh when Albertanus was born, and Brescia also shared in the popular religious movements of the age. The city was ruled by two strong reform-minded bishops during the period of Albertanus's youth and early manhood. Bishop Albert, who came from Reggio in Emilia (and who participated in the Fifth Crusade and went on to become Latin Patriarch of Antioch), struggled vigorously against local powers, lay and ecclesiastical, that threatened his rights as bishop. He was also known for his opposition to heresy. His successor, the Dominican prior Guala, originally from Bergamo, was also committed to reform of the church in Brescia. He too met opposition from a segment of the local powers. Albertanus must certainly have had views on these matters, but he has almost nothing to say about them.

Albertanus found himself caught in the tension between the demands of the community and the aspirations of the individual. Safeguarding the individual from the perils of society provides one of the central themes of his writing. As we will see, he was a profound student of the Roman philosopher Seneca, whose own withdrawal from the world and social ambivalences and fears reverberated in Albertanus's own experience. Albertanus's reading of Saint Augustine's *City of God* likewise reinforced this same concern. Confronted as he was with the violence and danger of the unstable society of communal Italy, Albertanus sought ways to transform that society, to create a true community. Of course, such a desire was neither new nor original. He lived, however, in a period before the availability of translations of Aristotle's ethics and politics, which would transform the political and social theories of the late thirteenth and fourteenth centuries. His own education, little as we know of it, reveals him to be a product of the twelfth century. His task then was to forge something from the scant materials of his education and from his experience that would enable him and his contemporaries to create that happiness (*beata vita*) he found idealized in Seneca and which he may also have found elements of in Saint Augustine.[35] In the process of doing this, he produced new insights from his sources and his experiences that enabled him to build bridges between twelfth-century moralism and the new social theories that would emerge in the latter part of the thirteenth century.

The chapters that follow move from the social matrix of Albertanus's Brescia to his development of a body of ideas about the consensual basis for organization of a just and happy society. Albertanus set forth a plan with that goal in mind. It is the nature of that plan that we will explore in his writings. Our aim is not to show that his ideas reshaped medieval and Renaissance social and political thought, but that they illustrate one way in which that process began to occur, combining elements drawn from religious reform movements, the increasing professionalism of Italian communal society, and the twelfth-century moralist tradition.

Voices like that of Albertanus are rare. All too often, as has been the case with him, they are ignored or relegated to a secondary level. The study of political and social thought has traditionally emphasized the importance and originality of ideas rather than the processes of their creation. Indeed, the study of political and social theory has been akin to a genealogy of the history of ideas.[36] Major figures from Plato to Machiavelli and Locke furnish the issues that are discussed and establish their limits. It is not my purpose to deny the value of this approach, which has often brought rich results, but to show how much more we can learn by probing the confrontation between the social and intellectual worlds.

The chief problem that this effort faces in the writings of Albertanus of Brescia stems from their nature as moral treatises and their consequent lack of historical context. The very elements that mark Albertanus as a theoretician raise obstacles to understanding the relationship of his ideas to political and social realities. The real world of concrete experience and specific institutions finds little place in his writings. He does not draw on the *exempla* of history. He was the product of a century intensely present oriented; the past had little impact on the writings of the thirteenth-century scholastics. Even the writing of history itself was more present oriented than had previously been the case. Theology and law had gained dominance over history. In their wake came a great stress on theoretical knowledge. Albertanus, though a twelfth-century man in so many ways, reflected these changes. Even if we cast his writings in traditional terms, we must recognize the degree to which they bridged the humanistic interests of the twelfth century and the paradigmatic tendencies of the thirteenth century. If Albertanus missed greatness as an original thinker, it was not because he lacked originality but because he may have been too original.

Notes

1. David M. Walker, *The Oxford Companion to Law* (Oxford, 1980), has provided the following brief definition of *causidicus*: "A term for the professional pleaders at Rome, who were not scholarly lawyers and indeed rather despised legal learning but orators, knowing only enough law to understand the advice they got from the jurisconsults." Aldo Checchini, "Un giudice del secolo decimoterzo: Albertano da Brescia," *Atti del reale istituto veneto di scienze, lettere ed arti* 71:2 (1911–12), 1423–95, discusses the meaning of *causidicus* in the thirteenth and fourteenth centuries (1429–31), basing his view that they served as legal counselors and assessors in part on quotations from Albertanus's own works. I believe that, with some allowance for a greater role of *causidici* as legal advisers, the definition advanced by Walker probably describes the thirteenth-century *causidicus*.

For a general introduction to the history of Brescia in this period, see Enzo Abeni, *La storia bresciana: Il frammento e l'insieme*, 4 vols. (Brescia, 1987) 2:338–56, which is largely based on *Storia di Brescia* vol. 1. Albertanus relates his role in the siege of Gavardo in his first treatise, cited here in the transcription made by Sharon Hiltz, "*De amore et dilectione Dei et proximi et aliarum rerum et de forma vitae:* An Edition," edited by Sharon Hiltz (Ph.D. diss., University of Pennsylvania, 1980), 289. On the disloyalty of Gavardo, see Alfredo Bosisio, "Brescia ai tempi di Federico II (1220–1250)," *Storia di Brescia* 1:655–76, cf. 670.

2. One of the serious problems in studying the writings of Albertanus of Brescia is the lack of modern critical editions. The Hiltz edition of the *De amore* is based chiefly on a single manuscript, Latin MS. 107, in the University of Pennsylvania Library. Thor Sundby edited the *De doctrina dicendi et tacendi,* under the title *De arte loquendi et tacendi,* in his *Della vita e delle opere di Brunetto Latini* (Florence, 1884), 479–506. I cite it as *De doctrina.* He also edited the *Liber consolationis et consilii* (Copenhagen, 1873). Monsignor Luigi F. Fè d'Ostiani edited Albertanus's Genoese sermon, *Sermone inedito di Albertano, giudice di Brescia* (Brescia, 1874), and Marta Ferrari edited his four Brescian sermons in *Sermones quattuor.* All of these editions are helpful, but all suffer because of their use of inferior manuscripts. In the preparation of this study, I have tried to make up for these deficiencies by comparing texts with various manuscripts. Those which have been most helpful have been Vatican City, BAV, Vat. Lat. 991 and 993, which include all of the treatises and the sermons. They date from the thirteenth and fourteenth centuries respectively. I have also consulted Milan, Biblioteca Ambrosiana, B. 40. Sup., and Florence, Biblioteca Riccardiana, 770, both of the thirteenth century. None of these are listed in the appendix prepared by Sharon Hiltz for her dissertation. I have also consulted Pavia, Biblioteca Universitaria, 235, which Hiltz does list. On the whole, I found her work very helpful and sincerely appreciate her efforts.

3. H.-B. 2:2, 926–28. Huillard-Bréholles refers to Albertanus as a Brescian judge in synopsizing this document. Most likely, he is recording the text of the document, but that is not entirely clear. Still, this terminology does not mean that Albertanus was a lawyer.

4. Aldo Checchini, "Un giudice," 1423–95. Ugo Vaglia, *Memorie illustri bresciani* (Brescia, 1958), 58–61, and Cesare Trebeschi, "Albertano da Brescia," *Uomini di Brescia,* ed. Fausto Balestrini (Brescia, 1987), 96–109, show the continued popular interest in Albertanus.

5. Albertanus gave this form of his name in the *explicit* to the *De amore* (Hiltz, "*De amore,*" 289). Likewise, the *De doctrina dicendi et tacendi* (Sundby, *De doctrina,* 506) and the *Liber consolationis et consilii* (Sundby, *Liber,* 127) contain similar information. However, his name appears in various other documents either with or without a reference to the church or quarter of Santa Agata. For example, *LP* 19:118–22 (1 February 1227) lists him simply as Albertanus. On the other hand, a document of 13 August 1249 (Milan, Archivio di Stato, Fondi religiosi, SS. Cosmo e Damiano, Cart. 65) calls him "Domino Albertano, judice de Sancta Agata" but refers to a charter drawn up in 1236 by "Albertanum de Porta" as notary and attested by Frederick II. Since Albertanus is a rare name in this region, we are left with the possibility that Albertanus practiced as a notary and used the form

Albertanus de Porta in this document. We are also confronted with the unique form of his title, "judge of Saint Agatha." In still another document, we find "Albertanus de pluvethiciis," which seems to be a corruption for the *pieve* of Saint Agatha (*LP* 19:708 [1233]).

6. *Sermones quattuor*, 63. "Et hoc vidi meis temporibus, qui in hac professione plusquam viginti quattuor annis exercitatus sum."

7. *LP* 19:122, 152–54, 165–66.

8. *LP* 19:708. "Inquisitio possessionum comunis Brixie occupatorum et in civitate et suburbis et clausis et Monte dennio." Albertanus served as counselor in this *Inquisitio*.

9. Hiltz, "*De amore*," 289.

10. *Sermone inedito*, 33.

11. Cinzio Violante, "La chiesa bresciana dall'inizio del secolo XIII al dominio veneto," *Storia di Brescia* 1:1064–1124, esp. 1094–98.

12. *Annales Parmenses maiores*, MGHSS 18:676; Ex Mathei Parisiensis, *Cronicis maioribus*, MGHSS 28:368. On Emmanuel, cf. Violante, *Storia di Brescia* 1:1092, and Ferdinand Gregorovious, *History of the City of Rome in the Middle Ages*, 8 vols. (London, 1903–12) 5:1, 319–21; *Codice diplomatico del senato romano dal MCXLIV al MCCCXLVII*, ed. Franco Bartaloni *Fonti per la storia d'Italia*, vol. 87; (Rome, 1947), 214–16. On Berardus, cf. Ferdinando Ughelli, *Italia Sacra*, 2d ed, 9 vols. in 8. Venice, 1717–22. (Reprint, Nendeln, Liecht., 1970) 4:550.

13. *LP* 19:677, 687.

14. *Moralium*. See also the interesting discussion in John Baldwin, *Masters, Princes, and Merchants: The Social Views of Peter the Chanter and His Circle*, 2 vols. (Princeton, 1970) 1:xi–xv. From other points of view, this issue has been developed in numerous works. See for example Hans Baron's classic article, "Franciscan Poverty and Civic Wealth as Factors in the Rise of Humanistic Thought," *Speculum* 13 (1938): 1–37, especially p. 3, on which he discusses the views of Albertanus. Although treating chiefly a somewhat later period, Lester Little's *Religious Poverty and the Profit Economy in Medieval Europe* (Ithaca, 1978) contributes substantially to our understanding of the changes that occurred in moral science.

15. The best works on the twelfth-century Senecan tradition are Leighton Reynolds, *The Medieval Tradition of Seneca's Letters* (London, 1965), and Klaus-Dieter Nothdurft, *Studien zum Einfluss Senecas auf die Philosophie und Theologie des Zwölften Jahrhundert* (Leiden, 1963). See also Claudia Villa, "La tradizione delle 'Ad Lucilium' e la cultura di Brescia dall'età carolingia ad Albertano," *Italia medioevale e umanistica* 12 (1969): 9–51, as well as the insightful comment of Gillian R. Evans, *Old Arts and New Theology* (Oxford, 1980), 21.

16. *Dei trattati morali di Albertano da Brescia volgarizzamento fatto nel 1268 da Andrea da Grosseto*, ed. Francesco Selmi (Bologna, 1873); *Soffredi del Grathia's Uebersetzung der philosophischen Traktate Albertano's von Brescia*, ed Gustav Rolin (Leipzig, 1898). For other Italian translations, see Nicola Zingarelli, "I trattati di Albertano da Brescia in dialetto veneziano," *Studi di letteratura italiana* 3 (1901): 151–92, and, more particularly, Saverio Panunzio, "Il codice Bargiacchi del volgarizzamento italiano del *Liber consolationis et consilii* di Albertano de Brescia," *Studi di Filologia Romanza offerti a Silvio Pellegrini* (Padua, 1971), 377–419; see esp.

378–79. For French translations, see Mario Roques, "Traductions françaises des traités moraux d'Albertano de Brescia," *Histoire literaire de la France* 37 (1936–38): 488–506. For other translations, see J. Knight Bostock, *Albertanus Brixiensis in Germany; Being an Account of the Middle High German Translations from his Didactic Treatises* (London, 1924), 10–11. Although Albertanus's works were well known in England, if one can trust the number of manuscripts found in English libraries, the only example of a translation is indirect, namely, Chaucer's "Tale of Melibee."

17. Brunetto Latini, *Li livres dou tresor*, ed. Francis J. Carmody (Berkeley, Cal., 1948), 236–45. See also Thor Sundby, *Della vita*, 171–77.

18. Santino Caramella, "Dante e Albertano da Brescia," *Studi letterari: Miscellanea in onore di Emilio Santini* (Palermo, 1956), 87–94.

19. Conrad Mainzer, "Albertano of Brescia's *Liber Consolationis et Consilii* as a Sourcebook of Gower's *Confessio Amantis*," *Medium Aevum* 47 (1978): 88–89. Chaucer adapted his version from that made by the French Dominican Renaut de Louhans in 1336 or 1337 (Roques, "Traductions françaises," 503).

20. Ibid., 502–3; *Le ménagier de Paris*, 2 vols. (Paris, 1816) 1:186–236.

21. Maria Corti, "Le fonti del *Fiore di virtù* e la teoria della 'Nobiltà' nel duecento," *Giornale storico della letteratura italiana* 71 (1959): 1–82.

22. Hiltz, "*De amore*," 290–325, lists more than three hundred manuscripts for this period, but my own research suggests that this number is far too low. Indeed, the final number may exceed five hundred manuscripts, which would place Albertanus among the most popular medieval authors. For example, there are only about sixty manuscripts of Pope Innocent III's sermons, though there are more than six hundred of his *De miseria condicionis humanae* (Athens, Ga., 1978), 3.

23. For a list of early printed editions, see *Sermone inedito*, 17–30.

24. See notes 2–21 above for bibliographical citations.

25. Only one of these sermons, the last (*Sermones quattuor*, 55) is dated, to 1250. Gérard G. Meersseman, "Il manuale dei penitenti di Brescia," *Ordo Fraternitatis*, I:410–50; for Albertanus, see his "Predicatori laici nelle confraternite medievali," *Ordo Fraternitatis* 3:1273–89.

26. Checchini, "Un giudice," 1431–44 and 1455–95.

27. Marta Ferrari, "Intorno ad alcuni sermoni inediti di Albertano da Brescia," *Atti del istituto veneto di scienze, lettere ed arti* 109 (1950–51): 69–93.

28. Cf. the mention of Albertanus among the pre-humanists by Francesco Novati, cited in Paul O. Kristeller, *Iter Italicum* I:297; Caramella, "Dante e Albertano da Brescia," 87; for Florence, see Charles T. Davis, *Dante's Italy and Other Essays* (Philadelphia, 1984).

29. Roberto Weiss, *Il primo secolo del umanesimo* (Rome, 1949); Giuseppe Billanovich, *I primi umanisti e le tradizioni dei classici italiani* (Freiburg, Switz., 1953); *Renaissance Humanism: Foundations, Forms, and Legacy*, ed. Albert Rabil, Jr., 3 vols. (Philadelphia, 1988).

30. Reynolds, *The Medieval Tradition*, 100; Villa, "La tradizione delle 'Ad Lucilium,'" 28–34. See note 15 above.

31. Analysis of the sources used by Albertanus suggests that he made little use of Italian materials. For the most part, he relied upon classical and early medieval sources, as well as the Old and New Testaments. When he did use

twelfth-century sources, they were chiefly moral treatises of non-Italian origin, such as the *Moralium dogma philosophorum* or the *Disciplina clericalis* of Petrus Alphonsi (Berkeley, Cal., 1977). Checchini has argued that Albertanus was influenced, especially in the *De doctrina dicendi et tacendi*, by Bolognese rhetoricians like Boncompagna da Signa (Checchini, "Un giudice," 1422–43). However, his major source for rhetoric is clearly Alcuin. Albertanus's use of sources raises the question whether he had studied extensively at either Bologna or Padua. These points are discussed in greater detail in later chapters.

32. Mainzer, "Albertano," 88–89. Corti, "Le fonti del *Fiore di virtù*," 1–82; Charles Owen, "The Tale of Melibee," *The Chaucer Review* 7 (1973): 267–80; Paul Olson, *The Canterbury Tales and the Good Society* (Princeton, 1986); Gardner Stillwell, "The Political Meaning of Chaucer's 'Tale of Melibee,'" *Speculum* 19 (1944): 433–44.

33. Hiltz, "*De amore*," 65–78; *Sermones quattuor*, 30. "Et liberare debemus pro posse pauperes a potentibus, ad exemplum Domini, de quo dicit propheta quod 'liberavit pauperem a potente; pauperem cui non erat adjutor'." Vatican City, BAV, Vat. Lat. 991:quia in place of quod.

34. Hiltz, "*De amore*," 195.

35. The concept of *beata vita*, translated as happiness, is derived by Albertanus from Seneca, as is clear from the reference in the *De amore et dilectione Dei* (Hiltz, "*De amore*," 102) and the discussion in Chapter 2 below, esp. note 4. Albertanus may also have encountered the term in his reading of Saint Augustine's *City of God* (bk. 19, chap. 4), however, where the context makes clear that Augustine is thinking of *beata vita* in terms of eternal life, rather than life in this world. Albertanus's *beata vita* retains its Senecan context and meaning. The idea of the pursuit of happiness is connected with his emphasis on the potential for improvement in earthly society, which forms one of the major themes of his work and of this study.

36. Quentin Skinner, "Political Philosophy," in *The Cambridge History of Renaissance Philosophy*, ed. Charles Schmitt (Cambridge, 1988), 389–452, esp. 412–15; Brian Tierney, *Religion, Law, and the Growth of Constitutional Thought, 1150–1650* (Cambridge, 1983). These works reflect, to some degree, the dissatisfaction with traditional approaches. See also J. G. A. Pocock, *The Machiavellian Moment: Florentine Political Thought and the Atlantic Republican Tradition* (Princeton, 1975) and his *Politics, Language, and Time* (New York, 1971).

1. The Structure of Violence in Albertanus's Brescia

IN A PASSAGE that has long stirred the popular imagination, Jacob Burckhardt contrasted medieval man, who "knew himself only in terms of race, *Volk*, party, corporation, family" with the new man, who "becomes an intellectual individual and recognizes himself as such." This latter man Burckhardt identifies with that power developed to the highest degree in the individuality of the Italian tyrants and the *condottieri* of the Renaissance.[1] Thus the linking of individualism and power, which the nineteenth century bequeathed in so many forms and concepts to our own, gained a political meaning that would help to shape fundamental views about individualism. In the long run, this identification of individualism and power has stirred profound moral reactions and aroused us to think again and again about the ways in which society might protect itself against the over-mighty. In the early thirteenth century, Albertanus of Brescia recognized that it was not so much the powerful who stood alone as it was the weak.[2] In a certain sense, true individuals were those whose weakness isolated them. The great dilemma thus posed was not, it seemed, that medieval society suffered a lack of individualism but that the rich and powerful were better organized to work together than were the poor and weak.

The Brescia of Albertanus was not unique as a laboratory of social and political relationships in the early thirteenth century. But it was unique as the chief practical laboratory in which Albertanus could contemplate those problems that would consume his efforts during the last decade or so of his life. A superficial glance at the history of Brescia's commune in the twelfth and thirteenth centuries confirms many similarities with other north Italian communes; a more intense examination reveals not merely differences, but also suggests that much recent discussion on the history of the thirteenth-century communes has been overly focused on issues in recent historiography rather than on the realities of internal development in the period.[3] In the case of Brescia, it is especially important to reexamine the social and political life of the commune if we are to understand the unique qualities of the experience that influenced Albertanus and helped to shape his ideas.

Thirteenth-century Brescia was drawn into the orbit of Milanese politics. In fact, the city, with its castello, set into the hillside overlooking the rich plain reaching southward to the Po, and with its back against the foothills of the Alps, represented the extreme eastern reach of Lombardy; in the fifteenth century Brescia would come within the orbit of Venice, to remain there until the eighteenth century. Unlike Milan and Verona, both of which controlled entrances to important Alpine passes, Brescia dominated only a lesser route along Lake Garda to Trent. Yet the city was not without significance. By the early thirteenth century, Brescian territory stretched across the heights of the *pre-Alpi* from Iseo to Toscolano, then southward along the shore of Garda to Desenzano and the River Oglio. To the west, its territory followed more or less the route of the Oglio past Soncino north to Adro and Iseo. These were not fixed boundaries. In the south and southwest, the Brescians sometimes moved across the Oglio, and the Cremonese, their major enemies in that area, also pushed across the river. In the northwest, Bergamo opposed Brescian expansion, though during most of our period, it posed little immediate danger.[4]

The major threat to Brescia during the first half of the thirteenth century came from Ezzelino da Romano, lord of Verona, who allied himself with the Emperor Frederick II during the 1230s in order to further his ambitious plan to build a state in northeastern Italy. Against this backdrop, Brescia came to play an important role in the politics of the Lombard League in support of Milan. Ultimately, these political struggles polarized around two political parties, the Guelphs and the Ghibellines, which during the second half of the thirteenth century would be identified as the party of the church and the party of the pro-imperial opposition.[5] Historians have usually regarded the former as a popular party composed of middle-class elements while the latter was dominated by members of the nobility. But these neat categories have broken down in the face of mounting evidence that the parties were remarkably similar in social and economic terms. Moreover, attempts to view their formation in ideological terms have suffered setbacks from studies that suggest that local interests and power relationships were fundamental in the emergence of political factions and parties.[6]

It has become increasingly clear that the first half of the thirteenth century was extremely important to the development of political parties in communal Italy. Brescia shared in these general developments in a special way because of its importance in the Lombard League. For this reason, there has been a strong tendency for Brescian scholars to view the earlier history of political factionalism and communal government in light of these later developments.[7] Brescia has been made to conform to the pattern shaped by concerns about the great issues that dominated external relations, but internal factors have not yet received adequate attention.

Another important feature of communal development in central and northern Italy was the effort of cities to control the *contado,* to impose urban power over rural lords often to force them to enter into the commune. Expansion into the *contado* brought conflict with numerous elements and sometimes resulted in unusual allies. Although conflict of communes with bishops, who often had large holdings in the *contado,* often erupted during this expansion, there were notable cases, as at Florence in the early thirteenth century, where cooperation between commune and bishop marked this process. Likewise alliances between the communes and rural lords were not exceptional, though conflict might appear more usual. Seldom did expansion proceed at a regular pace or in a single direction. Very often, the interests of various groups clashed as a result of circumstances arising from this process. Like so many communes in this period, Brescia succeeded in increasing substantially the rich agricultural lands under its control, thus ensuring food supplies for its growing population.[8]

Along with virtually every other city or town in northern Italy, one might even say in Europe, in the early thirteenth century, Brescia was bursting its seams. The main indication of this growth in Brescia was the building of a new set of walls enclosing a much larger area during the 1230s and 1240s. At the same time, a disastrous earthquake that destroyed much of the city in 1222 inspired the construction of a grand municipal building, the *Broletto,* with a large piazza.[9] The documents make clear that considerable urban planning accompanied these works. They hint, too, that some of the leading families owned property that was purchased by the commune to carry out this construction. The rich families of the town, most of whom were also rich families of the countryside, grew more prosperous during these years, and the move to the city seems to have also enriched some families of lesser status. Needless to say, however, there was no more equality in the distribution of this new wealth than there had been in the case of old money and lands. In fact, increased prosperity brought additional reasons for conflict among the rich and powerful.

In its cultural and religious life, Brescia has received less attention than centers like Milan and Padua.[10] Unlike Padua, Brescia was not the home of a university in the thirteenth century. Its most singular claim to fame lay in its role as the home of the twelfth-century reformer and heretic Arnold of Brescia.[11] Unfortunately for Brescia, the association with Arnold seems to have influenced later generations to view it as a haven for heretics. But Brescia was also an important center of religious reform in the early thirteenth century. Its bishops, Albert of Reggio and Guala of Bergamo, were among the leading Italian promoters of reform during the first half of the thirteenth century, cooperating closely with Innocent III, Honorius III, Gregory IX, and Innocent IV. Shortly after their foundation, the Dominicans were established in Brescia. In fact, Guala was installed as their prior in 1221 by Cardinal Ugolino of Ostia, Honorius III's legate in northern Italy and later Pope Gregory IX. The exact date for the arrival of the Franciscans is not certain, but they occupied the church of San Giorgio Martire for some years prior to 1250. Brescia was also an important center for the Humiliati, who had several houses along the river to the south of the town and enjoyed the patronage of a number of important families, including the Gambara and the de Madiis (Maggi), both of whom had ties to Albertanus of Brescia. The charitable life of the town flourished. Brescians supported hospitals for the sick and poor as well as a number of monasteries and convents.[12]

In sum, Brescia was a middling-sized, prosperous provincial town, whose population can roughly be estimated at less than fifty thousand. But it was a historic city that could, if it wished, glory in its Roman roots. Its nobility, drawn from the surrounding countryside, dominated its political life; there was a small professional class, of which Albertanus was a member, and some trade and industry. But the merchants of Brescia were in no position to challenge the nobles; only the divisions within the nobility made it possible for other groups to exercise limited political influence. At Brescia, politics centered on the aristocracy. These families set the tone of social and political life in the commune. It was from their midst that political factions emerged. The late twelfth and early thirteenth centuries did not experience the stability of a party system. We cannot, however, regard politics at this time as merely a matter of temporary alliances. Rather, we must search for those elements that first gave shape to the various factions. Among these we will also find some that formed the basis for the more stable political parties that came into existence in the second half of the thirteenth century and later, parties that coalesced around the terms *parte Guelfa* and *parte Ghibellina*. These elements reveal the seams where factions were brought together to form larger parties and where they might possibly fracture only to re-form along new lines. At Brescia, evidence of party formation helps us trace the development of political factions and the reasons for conflict among these factions. However, we need to keep in mind that our purpose in reexamining the meaning of party and the causes of conflict is limited to gaining a better understanding of the society in which Albertanus lived and worked. For this reason, we will focus on elements that relate to his experience as revealed in surviving documents and his writings.

The older approach to study of a literary or political figure was to focus on the individual and to relate him to the context of his society. While that might be justifiable for biography, particularly for the life of a major personality, there is always the danger that, in seeing the world or even a small part of it through the eyes of a single person, we may so distort the result as to make it almost meaningless. For Albertanus, such an approach would merely lead to a slender catalog of his participation, in various guises, in the political and economic life of the commune.[13] While the extant documents are valuable and tell us much more than has previously been gleaned about Albertanus, they provide only the slightest context for understanding the matrix in which his social thought developed. Therefore, in the present chapter, we propose to concentrate on the reconstruction of those aspects of Brescian society that are most closely related to the themes of his writings and that impinge on the concerns that motivated him. Such concentration will help us understand how he fit within his own world and how the limited world of Brescia and its neighbors fit within the history of communal Italy. This is a preliminary step to the effort to put Albertanus's writings into the context of moral and political literature of the thirteenth century.

The temptation to read political events in the communes in terms of a papal-imperial or a communal-imperial tension has its origin in the sources themselves, though it was given a definitive shape in nineteenth-century historiography, which saw these events in terms of an ideological struggle between the medieval papacy and the empire. This version was, however, far removed from the origins of political factions and parties as presented in early thirteenth-century sources. Under the year 1194, for example, the anonymous author of the *Annales brixiensis* noted that peace had been negotiated between Milan and Brescia "and their party," and Cremona, Bergamo, Pavia, Lodi, and Como, and their party "through

Tuxardus, the *missus* of the Emperor."[14] Quite obviously, the author had in mind an imperial role rather different from that which pitted the Lombard towns against the empire. The emperor was, of course, very often a party to struggles rather than a sovereign attempting to bring an end to violence through mediation; but despite the numerous occasions on which emperors had descended into Italy with arms to support one group of magnates and cities against their enemies, there were others when they attempted to mediate disputes. This is what the representative of Henry VI was attempting in 1194. On another occasion, in 1210, Otto IV arranged a peace between political factions at Brescia.[15] Mediation was far more common and more significant than most historians have recognized. The role of the negotiator, though the terminology remains quite fluid during this period, became increasingly professionalized. Judges, *nuntii*, ambassadors, consuls, and podestàs all took part in the mediation process, as did many lesser officials, among whom we should mention the *causidici*, the professional legal counselors to whom Albertanus belonged.

Political factions in Brescia during the late twelfth and early thirteenth centuries were referred to by a number of different names. The term *milites* is most common. Not surprisingly, *milites* have usually been viewed in economic terms, even in those accounts that eschew class interpretation, for, the *milites* were members of the economic and social elite.[16] But *milites* was primarily a military term, and too little attention has been paid to that aspect of political and social life. The *milites* represented a form of coercive power essential to a society in which political fragmentation was the order of the day.[17] They were an essential, if dangerous, element in the world in the period between the decay of the Carolingian Empire and the formation of communal states.

Milites were already prominent in the urban conflicts that erupted in Italy in the late eleventh century. With the emergence of the communes, they came to play a key role both in urban politics and those of the *contado*. The origins of political factions and parties were at least to some degree influenced by those processes of social reconstruction that clustered around the religious reform movement of the eleventh century. Cinzio Violante made this connection a generation ago in his studies on the Milanese Pataria.[18] But few urban historians have followed his lead. The reform program profoundly affected the social order at almost every level. In the name of restoring the liberty of the church, it questioned almost every other right and jurisdiction, religious or secular, in medieval society.

The twelfth century saw further growth of the movement on the part of bishops and monasteries to regain lost rights and properties.[19] Historians have usually emphasized that the main thrust of these efforts was against the laity, particularly the aristocracy. In fact, much conflict broke out between bishops and monasteries and bishops and chapters, that is, those clergy who served the cathedral and often controlled substantial amounts of property as well as enjoying considerable power at the bishop's expense and indeed among clergy and laity generally.[20] In an age where litigation grew more quickly than new lawyers could be trained at the emerging law schools, the reform movement provided an impetus to re-examine the foundations of virtually the whole social fabric.

Moreover, there was no way in which the interests of the laity could be separated from those of the clergy. In a conflict between a bishop and a monastery, for example, the vassals of each became parties to the dispute because their livelihoods and those of their descendants were involved in the outcome. Likewise, those who dwelled within the cities, many of them members of the nobility, had interests in the countryside and were drawn into the conflicts that arose there. Thus, the *milites* of town and countryside, their loyalties divided, were factionalized by their economic interests and their ties to superiors. Sworn associations, or communes, aimed to protect those rights that the cities had gained by purchase, war, free gift, or coercion from other contenders, including other groups living within each city. Factionalism represented a political response to threats posed by those supporting as well as those questioning the traditional order of society.

In Brescia, the political factions that figure so prominently in the *Annales brixienses* were dominated by the *milites*.[21] True enough, the annals record a conflict in 1196 between the *milites* and the *paraticos*, the knights and the members of the craft guilds, which would seem to be a classic example of a class conflict, and it may have been.[22] But this type of conflict was overshadowed by the long-running dispute between the bishops of Brescia and their vassals and the abbots of Leno and theirs over disputed jurisdictions that involved the commune of Brescia and its claims in the areas south of the city.[23] For example, the formation of the *Societas Sancti Faustini*, no doubt related to the church of that name, and its dispute with the *milites* in 1200 obscures the fact that the aristocratic pretensions of the *Societas* were every bit as strong as those of the so-called *milites*.[24] In fact, the leaders of the two factions were closely related. Alberto, count of Casaloldo, who headed the *milites*, was a cousin of Narisius of Montechiari, who was a leader of the *Societas* and who was elected podestà by the

Societas. The *Societas* seems to have been chiefly a means of mobilizing the Brescian *popolo* in support of a minority faction among the nobles.[25] In 1207, a party led by Count Alberto and Vifredus Confanonerius entered Leno, the seat of a wealthy monastery south of Brescia, after they had been expelled from the city by a party led by Count Narisius, Pizius, and Jacobus Confanonerius. The party led by Jacobus, in alliance with the sons of Bocacius de Manere, attempted unsuccessfully to dislodge the *pars Alberti*.[26] Although the *Annales* do not directly mention either the bishop or the abbot of Leno, who had been at odds with one another, it seems clear that the communes and societies formed at this time acted chiefly in alliance with the bishop while the *milites* represented a faction led by vassals of the monastery of Leno. This view finds support in the fact that in 1209, the abbot of Leno entered the monastery with the support of Guido Lupus, who had assumed leadership of the *milites* from the exiled faction, that is, those who had formerly been identified as the *pars Alberti*.[27]

What gave consistency and coherence to the parties was not the leadership of individuals alone, as some have suggested, but the underlying interests of the group. Particularly striking is the fact that families frequently split, suggesting that these interests cut across family lines. These divisions were sometimes represented by those who had remained in the countryside as opposed to those who had taken up residence in the city, but this situation could change with the circumstances of individuals.[28] Another indication of the underlying coherence of the parties lay in the use of the term *milites leonenses* to identify the faction that supported the abbot.[29]

If jurisdictional disputes were important in the development of factions, so too were the efforts of bishops and others to recruit supporters in particular geographical areas. The numerous Martinengo family had ties to both Brescia and Bergamo.[30] Their ancestral seat rested on the border between the two cities. However, the family was more closely identified with Bergamo in the twelfth century. It was only late in the century, as the bishops of Brescia sought vassals to increase their control of the areas west of the city, that the Martinengo became more deeply involved in the affairs of Brescia. They soon became a critical factor in the effort of the bishop and his allies to strengthen their overall position against the *milites leonenses* and their allies.[31]

In 1214, Loderengo de Martinengo became podestà in Brescia for three years with the support of the recently elected bishop, Albert of Reggio, who was anxious to resolve disputes in the city.[32] Albert, who was closely guided by the peace policies promoted by Pope Innocent III in preparation for the Fourth Lateran Council and the renewal of the crusade, had himself attempted to mediate between the factions.[33] Albert had failed to reconcile the sons of Bocacius with the two major factions, those within the city and those in exile. Loderengo, too, was largely unsuccessful, though the peace arranged between the *pars superior* and the *pars inferior*, names which referred to the upper and lower parts of the city, under pressure from Paganus, podestà of Cremona, indicates that external forces had been summoned once again to support one faction against another.[34] The new terminology also suggests that the geographical power bases of the two parties in the city served to identify them in the minds of the people.

We may find this new terminology misleading at first, since it seems to suggest a change in political parties. While there was some realignment of the parties, however, their composition seems to have remained essentially the same. On 22 December 1219, two members of the Brescian clergy travelled to Parma to invite Mattheus of Corregia to take the office of podestà of Brescia at the invitation of the current podestà, probably Loderengo.[35] Mattheus clearly had the support of Bishop Albert and the commune, which in Brescia tended to support the bishop. But the close cooperation between Pope Honorius III and the German king, Frederick II, who was soon to enter Italy on his way to Rome for coronation as emperor, also meant that the empire and the papacy shared a common interest in promoting internal peace in the north Italian communes. For the time being, local parties could not look to a divided papal/imperial leadership to support their cause.

The Brescian *milites,* who had regularly allied themselves to Cremona, had sought imperial support, as had the abbots of Leno, to reinforce their position against the bishops of Brescia. The papacy too had usually supported the position of the abbots. Now, however, with Bishop Albert identified with the efforts of the papacy to promote the crusade there was a realignment. Pope and Emperor-elect supported Albert in his effort to bring peace to Brescia. Peace was essential in order to make the crusade possible. Mattheus of Corregia seemed to be the kind of leader who could bring peace. But the peace party at Brescia seems to have been too weak to secure control of the city and deliver it to him. The *milites* were able to exclude him and to elect their own podestà, Obertus de Gambara, one of the leading vassals of the abbot of Leno and a member of a family that had long supported efforts to exclude the bishop of Brescia from jurisdiction over the church of Gambara. The complexity of local politics becomes more manifest as we see the mounting forces opposed to the *milites*, including the papal legate, Cardinal Ugolino of Ostia; the Imperial chancellor, Conrad, Bishop of Metz; Bishop Albert, and their Brescian opposition.[36] The party of the *milites*, the *pars superior*, so known from its control of the upper city, found it essential to search for allies.

The internal political struggle in Brescia proceeded against this background. The Brescian *milites* found themselves charged with impeding the departure of a crusade. Amidst this struggle a new factor emerged to further complicate the factional conflict. At least as early as 1224, the charge was made that the *milites* were supporting heretics, were perhaps infected with heresy themselves.[37] Under the circumstances, the involvement of the papacy became more direct.

The charge of heresy against the *milites* and their followers is important for a number of reasons. In the first place, it has served to confirm the view of modern scholars that heresy was very prominent in Brescia in the late twelfth and thirteenth centuries. It has also demonstrated the potency of the charge of heresy as a weapon in the party politics of the thirteenth century. Moreover, it indicates the way in which political factions came together as a result of local needs but found themselves drawn into broader issues, in this instance because they were joined by the heretics, much as they were earlier drawn into the politics of the crusade. Somewhat surprising is the fact that the heretics were linked to the *milites* of the *pars superior*, rather than to their opponents who had more support among the *popolo* of the commune of Brescia, since most previous scholarship has linked heretics to the latter.[38] The Brescian experience need not be typical of other Lombard cities, but certain features raise questions that do not fit easily into current views of either Lombard politics or the place of heresy in Lombardy.

The accusation that heresy flourished in the Lombard communes, especially in Milan, needs serious study, not least because contemporary imperial, papal, and other sources seem to agree that heretics were both numerous and influential in the cities. Was heresy in Lombardy an urban phenomenon or was it more to be found in smaller places, scattered through the countryside? Recent research on heresy in Italy and elsewhere has cast serious doubts on older interpretations of heresy. Malcolm Lambert has observed that Cathar bishops in southern France tended to live in rural areas under the protection of members of the local nobility.[39] He also cites with approval studies of heresy in Italy in the fourteenth century that indicate it was strong in rural areas.[40] On the other hand, thirteenth-century Italian sources that tended to emphasize the importance of the cities as centers of heresy often reflected the views of papal and imperial propagandists who authored such charges.[41]

Padua identified the cause of Ezzelino da Romano with that of the heretics, a view widely shared among contemporary opponents of Ezzolino and his family.[42] But the Paduans also indicted Verona, Vicenza, and Treviso as centers of heresy while stressing their own freedom from taint. Of course, there was as much evidence of heresy in Padua as in these other towns in the early thirteenth century, but heresy was more easily found elsewhere. Even the great Saint Anthony was summoned to witness that Padua was free of heresy.

Brescia's reputation had already suffered near irreparable damage from association with Arnold of Brescia.[43] Whether or not Arnold was formally a heretic, he was widely believed to have taught heretical views and he certainly questioned ecclesiastical authority. He maintained that "neither clerics that owned property, nor bishops that had regalia, nor monks with possessions, could in any wise be saved."[44] But it was chiefly in Rome that Arnold carried on his activities and earned the reputation that led to his execution by the prefect of the city on charges of rebellion.[45] The charges of heresy that emerged in Brescia in the 1220s had no clear links to any earlier heretical group. On the other hand, the accusations provide a basis for intensive study of the role of heresy in local politics.

The promulgation of legislation against heretics by the Fourth Lateran Council in 1215 and by Frederick II on the occasion of his imperial coronation in 1220 was the beginning of a papal campaign to secure acceptance and enforcement of these laws by all the ecclesiastical and political authorities of northern Italy.[46] At the same time, the pope was under considerable pressure from the emperor and his supporters to promote political settlements between the empire and the communes as well as among the communes themselves, in order to release the emperor to fight in the crusade. Such support was also valuable as an adjunct of Frederick's policy for the restoration of imperial rights in northern Italy. Following the defeat of the crusader army at Damietta in Egypt in 1221, the papacy redoubled its efforts to secure a political climate favorable to a crusade led by the Emperor. On 4 May 1224, Honorius III wrote Bishop Albert of Brescia and Bishop William of Modena, ordering them to implement the decrees of the Fourth Lateran Council against heretics in Lombardy. At this stage, there is no reason to suspect that the pope was thinking of

Brescia in specific terms. His main concern was to carry out those reforms to which he and Frederick had committed themselves by the imperial legislation of 1220. That the timing of this measure was inspired in part by imperial pressure seems clear from the reference to the "civitates et alia loca Lombardiae,"[47] since these were a particular target of the imperial politicians. While the results of this letter are not clear, there can be little doubt that Bishop Albert saw the papal commission as ready-made to deal with the internal situation in Brescia itself.

As a result of a report from Albert, the pope addressed a letter on 11 September 1224 to the *milites* and *populus* of Brescia in which he deplored those (a considerable number) tainted with heresy and praised those supporting the bishop, asking that they aid their bishop in extirpating heresy.[48] The implications for local politics are obvious. Needless to say, the bishop required no urging to implement the papal advice. The alliance of papacy, bishop, and commune was much more effective than the efforts of the imperial chancellor or of the emperor himself, though Frederick had put the opposition to Mattheus of Corregia under the ban of the empire in order to maintain pressure.

Albert and his supporters triumphed in early 1225, even as Pope Honorius was ordering the bishop to destroy the towers and houses of the heretics in Brescia.[49] In this letter the pope referred to Brescia as a *domicilium hereticorum*, a homeland of heretics.[50] Despite the impression that this term has made on modern scholars, the pope added some information that has usually been overlooked. He stated that these heretics and their followers "recently erupted in such insanity," using their towers against the Catholics and even destroying churches and shouting blasphemies. Despite the term *domicilium hereticorum*, the letter actually refers to the actions of the leaders of the *milites* in the current political struggle, whose towers are then named: the Ugoni, the Oriani, the sons of the late Bocacius de Manerbio, and the Gambara. These are, of course, notable members of the *milites*. They are also members of those families with long ties to the monastery of Leno and a history of opposition to the bishops of Brescia.[51] The continuity of local politics thus helps to explain, in this case, the political involvement of heretics in Brescia.

Were there in fact heretics among the supporters of the *milites*? The answer to that question requires an examination of the composition of heretical groups within the district of Brescia. In spite of the words of Honorius III, there is little independent evidence for the presence of substantial numbers of heretics within Brescia itself. Even the reference to an individual heretic as "of Brescia" only suggests the possibility that a heretic was born there.[52] On the other hand, there is considerable evidence for the presence of groups of heretics, especially Cathars, in the district outside the city. The places mentioned as sheltering groups of heretics are Desenzano, on the southwest shore of Lake Garda; Mosio, the seat of the Ugoni counts; and Bagnolo, just to the north of Manerbio.[53] All of these places and the families identified with them are closely associated with the monastery of Leno. It seems clear that heresy was strongest, so far as we can now determine, in the rural towns where episcopal authority had long been in dispute and which lay on the route northward through the Alps. This is not to suggest, however, any simple relationship between episcopal-monastic conflict and development of heresy.

But the discontent that lay at the root of jurisdictional disputes did create conditions in which disaffected groups were more prepared to support heretical leaders, who seem to have often concentrated their efforts on just such fertile ground in the countryside. But among whom? Not, apparently, among the peasants, who would in any case have had little at stake, but among the professional class and the small landholders and their families, linked to the nobles by ties of patronage and economic support. These included notaries, artisans, and perhaps local officials. Beyond a doubt, heretics also made converts or found sympathizers among those of higher ranks, perhaps especially among upper-class women. In this instance, the bishop, recognizing the presence of heretics among the supporters of the *milites,* did not hesitate to use this fact against them. Perhaps the political position of the *milites* made them even more vulnerable to this charge at this time. At any rate, there is more than a small suspicion that most of the heretics in the area were dependents of the *milites* and enjoyed a measure of protection from them. Such heretics as were in the city may well have been brought there by members of this group.

We cannot completely deny that Brescia was a *domicilium hereticorum,* but we have raised doubts whether the original description was based on anything more than the heat of politics and the circumstances of the moment. It is also evident that politics at Brescia by 1225 had increasingly been drawn onto a broader stage. Still, the continuity of Brescian political parties seems to depend much more on local concerns than upon any ideological questions that emerged from the concerns of the papacy or the empire at this time. Even local opposition to imperial dominance of the commune was confused by the current cooperation of pope and emperor. However, as scholars have long recognized, the involvement of the

Brescian *milites* with heretics did not mean that they were themselves heretics. Actually, they moved rapidly to extricate themselves from what had become an untenable situation.

In mid July 1225, a group of Brescian *milites,* mostly nobles, arrived in Rome and put their case before the pope.[54] The resultant papal letter opened a new phase in the conflict. Claiming that they had been wrongly accused of heresy merely because some who had supported their party were heretics, the named individuals sought absolution from Pope Honorius III. They were Raymond, Count of Mosio; Raymond de Ugonibus; Tetoccius de Tetocciis; Fredericus de Lavellolongo; Matheus de Gambara; Joannes de Manervio; Ottolino Meleghette; and Bonaventura de Walando. Save for the last named, who was a notary, all were men of substance, though not necessarily leading members of their families.[55] Honorius recognized merit in their claim and ordered the bishops to assess penalties in proportion to guilt, and, where justified, to moderate his previous instructions to destroy the houses and towers of the guilty and to exact any other penalties the bishops might have ordered.

During the next year, negotiations continued. In May 1226, Honorius spoke of the reconciliation of the citizens of Brescia in order to promote tranquillity and peace in the city, again encouraging moderation in assessing penalties.[56] We can only suggest that the *milites* had found a somewhat sympathetic ear in Rome. In fact, as preparations for the emperor's departure on crusade lagged during 1226 and 1227 and as problems with other Lombard communes began to threaten papal plans, Honorius was more interested in ending conflicts than in perpetuating local grievances, even when such a serious matter as heresy was involved.[57] Quite clearly, the curia had decided to separate the political problems of Brescia from the issue of heresy.

The *milites* had gained something of a victory despite their defeat. Since there can be little doubt they were aware that some of their followers were heretics, including some dependents who had been heretics for a considerable period of time and had operated more or less openly out of Mosio, Desenzano, and other places under *milites'* control, the situation was even analogous to that in southern France.[58] Honorius's solution, if we may call it that, differed from that of his predecessor Innocent III in the case of southern France. The handling of the Brescian problem seems to mark a tentative step in the evolution of papal policy leading to the Inquisition, focusing on the heretics more than on the political leaders of the area. But there is no evidence that the commission of the bishops to extirpate heresy in Lombardy involved a formal process of inquisition. Actually, we have no evidence of the prosecution of any individual or group for heresy in Brescia save within the framework outlined by the pope. To some degree, at least, the problem of heresy at Brescia seems to have receded behind the political effort to secure a peace settlement between the factions.

But what of those who participated in this civil disorder against the bishop and the pope and who succeeded in displacing Mattheus of Corregia and replacing him with their own podestà, Obertus de Gambara? There is no evidence of any harsh or enduring penalties levied against them. Some of the evidence is not entirely conclusive, but the absence of testimony from letters and chronicles, as well as the more abundant documentary evidence for some of those named in Pope Honorius's letter, makes a strong case. Bonaventura de Walano (or de Wala), imperial notary, is first documented in January 1211 and last mentioned in a charter for the monastery of Santa Giulia in Brescia in 1227.[59] Ottolino "filius Domini Melchette" participated in an inquiry into land ownership in Mosio conducted on behalf of the commune.[60] He was one of the affected landholders. This was shortly after 1225, possibly in 1227, when Count Raymond de Mosio also took part in an inquest there.[61] Raymond de Ugonibus testified in a trial involving the commune of Asula in 1238 along with Fredericus de Lavellolongo.[62] Tetoccius de Tetocciis was a witness along with Albertanus—this is one of the early cases in which his name appears—in charters dealing with the sale of property for the new municipal building and its piazza in February 1227. In 1233, Tetoccius was one of two representatives from Brescia to the Lombard League.[63] In May 1251, Fredericus de Lavellolongo witnessed a peace treaty between Brescia and Bergamo along with Albertanus de Sancta Agatha.[64] Joannes de Manervio served as Brescian ambassador to Rome in 1232, dealing with the cardinals about an agreement with Frederick II.[65] Matheus of Gambara had earlier served as podestà of Brescia, but nothing is known of him after 1225.[66]

Not only did those accused of consorting with heretics survive, several remained politically influential. Moreover, the identification of Tetoccius, Fredericus, and Joannes as important figures in Lombard politics in opposition to the Emperor Frederick II after 1230, reflects yet another major shift in the politics of Brescia. Apparently, those who had joined the bishop, the pope, and the emperor in 1219 to support Mattheus of Corregia changed sides in the late 1230s, eventually supporting the Emperor Frederick II in his opposition to the papacy. On the other hand, the *milites* of the 1220s found themselves in alliance with the bishop and commune, as the core of the emerging Guelph party. They had become the dominant faction in the city. Interestingly, there is no more mention of heretics in their midst. Indeed, discussion of heretics in Brescia seems to have receded, to emerge only when Frederick II and his allies, the Da Romano family, were accused of consorting with heretics in the period after 1239.[67] Certainly, heresy remained a potent political issue. Nor is there reason to doubt that some heretics found it politic to support the imperial cause. But the "heretics" of the 1220s had been forgotten.

Study of the formation of political factions in Brescia provides strong evidence against any single explanation for their origin and development. Conflicts over local rights and jurisdictions engendered in part by the reform movement were important in providing continuity and consistency to geographically based parties such as the *milites leonenses*. We also need to recognize, however, that political factions often had roots in the countryside, in the clients and dependents of the powerful personages who provided their leaders. This has been illustrated by the evidence of the manner in which heretics became identified with the Brescian *milites*, found in the testimony of the letters of Pope Honorius III as well as in the result of studies showing that heretics were generally found in such places as Mosio, Desenzano, and Bagnolo, places under the control of the very families represented in the group labeled as heretics by Honorius III.

As subsequent chapters will make clear, Albertanus's conception of faction reflected just this kind of inter-personal familial situation. Read against the background of Brescian political experience at this time, and keeping in mind Albertanus's own connections with the leading faction in the city from the late 1220s, his writings reveal his concern with issues and attitudes that have appeared in this discussion. His quest for the foundations on which an orderly society might be built proceeds from concerns about his family, his colleagues, and his city that articulate authentic aspirations of the urban professional group to which he belonged.

In the years after 1226, when Albertanus de Sancta Agatha was establishing himself professionally in Brescia, the violence of communal politics became a matter of deep professional concern to the young *causidicus*, who was attempting to find means to resolve both public and private disputes in accordance with legal principles rather than knives, swords, spears, clubs, and rocks. Albertanus experienced factionalism directly. He identified with the commune and its interests throughout his public career.

Although it was impossible to remain totally outside of the party framework and still be a citizen, Albertanus seemed to have been a moderate in party politics. He stressed his professionalism in his writings; he lived that professionalism in his public life.

His identification with the commune, particularly with the emergent *milites*, is quite clear from the existing evidence. He was one of the earliest medieval voices to announce a new pursuit of happiness in this world as well as the world to come. His commitment to the commune and to voluntary association as the direction in which humans should move in their quest for a more perfect society places him in a tradition that would include the Machiavelli of the *Discourses* rather than the tyrants and princes Burckhardt saw as the heirs of the age of medieval city republics. Albertanus did not produce merely an early version of civic republicanism. He was also one of the first to recognize flaws within that tradition and to search for alternatives. It was his dissatisfaction which motivated and gave shape to the *De amore* in 1238.

Notes

1. Jacob Burckhardt, *Die Kultur der Renaissance in Italien*, 13th ed. (Leipzig, 1922), 99.

2. This theme is developed in *Liber consolationis et consilii* (Sundby, *Liber*, 97–99) and in the sermons (*Sermones quattuor*, 30). It seems to be implied by the way in which Albertanus dwells on the text, "tibi derelictus est pauper." It is treated more explicitly in the *Liber consolationis*, where he talks about the effects of wealth on power (98).

3. There is substantial literature on the communes that cannot be more than alluded to here. For a bibliography, cf. *Storia d'Italia*, ed. G. Galasso (Turin, 1981), vol. 4 only. John K. Hyde, *Society and Politics in Medieval Italy: The Evolution of Civil Life* (London, 1973) is a useful survey. More controversial is Lauro Martines, *Power and Imagination: City-States in Renaissance Italy* (New York, 1979). For recent work, see Daniel Waley, *The Italian City-Republics*, 3d ed. (London, 1988).

4. On Brescia, cf. *Storia di Brescia* 1, passim. Brescia has not attracted great interest among historians, but local scholarship has produced Jacopo Malvezzi (Jacobus Malvecius) whose *Chronicon* (*RISS* 14) marks the beginning of humanistic history in Brescia. Other writers of note are Elia Cavriolo, Federico Odorici, C. F. Bertoni, Luigi F. Fè d'Ostiani, R. Putelli, and Paolo Guerrini. Odorici's *Storie bresciane dai primi tempi sino all'età nostra*, 11 vols. (Brescia, 1853–65) is especially valuable for its publication of documents. The Odorici archive in the Biblioteca Queriniana has been catalogued by Rosa Zilioli Faden, *Catalogo inventariale dei manoscritti della raccolta Odorici* (Brescia, 1988).

5. Jacques Heers, *Parties and Political Life in the Medieval West* (Amsterdam, 1977).

6. Heers, *Parties and Political Life*, provides the most comprehensive discussion of the formation of medieval political parties to date, examining multiple causes as factors in their origin and development. I make no attempt to summarize his conclusions, but am indebted to his insights at various points in this discussion. Nevertheless, in what follows I suggest a rather different approach to political parties in Brescia from the one he has adopted.

7. Bosisio, *Storia di Brescia* 1:655–76.

8. Angelo Baronio, *Monasterium et populus: Per la storia del contado lombardo, Leno* (Brescia, 1984); Paolo Guerrini, *Una celebre famiglia lombarda: I conti di Martinengo* (Brescia, 1930), 107–76; Luigi F. Fè d'Ostiani, "I conti rurali bresciani del medio evo," *Archivio storico lombardo* 26 (1899): 5–55.

9. Such information as we have regarding the population of Brescia has been collected by Karl Julius Beloch, *Bevölkerungsgeschichte Italiens*, 3 vols. (Berlin, 1937–61) 3:121–41; *Annales brixienses, MGHSS* 18:818. Construction on the new city hall began in or shortly after 1227 (*LP* 19:118–22 [2 February 1227]), probably as a result of the earthquake of 1222, but the choice of site may have been influenced by this conflict. (See below, note 37.) Albertanus appears among the witnesses along with more than one hundred members of the Brescian nobility and the professions in several charters involving land sales for the Palazzo del Broletto during this period. Albertanus also witnesses a charter of sale by the de la Carzia family to the commune in November 1227. *LP* 19:152–54; Malvezzi, *Chronicon Brixianum, RISS* 14:900–902 on the earthquake and the Broletto palace.

10. For Padua, compare John K. Hyde, *Padua in the Age of Dante* (Manchester, 1966), 121–53. Hyde demonstrates the importance of university professors in the cultural and civic life of Padua.

11. George W. Greenaway, *Arnold of Brescia* (New York, 1978), 48–57.

12. Violante, *Storia di Brescia* 1:1064-1124; Alfredo Brontesi, "Guala, vescovo di Brescia," *Bibliotheca sanctorum* 7:412–19; Ferdinando Ughelli, *Italia sacra*, 2d ed., 9 vols. (Venice, 1717–22. Reprint, Nendeln, Liecht., 1970) 4:546–47.

13. On Albertanus, the best study is that by Marta Ferrari, "Intorno ad alcuni sermoni inediti di Albertano da Brescia," *Atti del istituto veneto di scienze, lettere ed arti* 109 (1950–51): 69–93, which summarizes work done previous to 1950. A more recent study is found in Anna Maria Finoli, "La cultura à Brescia nel medioevo," *Storia di Brescia* 1:971–97, esp. 990–93. Thor Sundby's essay on Albertanus (*Liber*, v–xxiv) remains useful.

14. *Annales brixiensis, MGHSS* 18:815. For further background cf. *Annales placentini guelfi, MGHSS* 18:423–24.

15. *Annales brixiensis, MGHSS* 18:817.

16. See for example Heers, *Parties and Political Life*, 29–32.

17. Ibid., 203–4 has an interesting discussion of the *milites gaudenti*, who undertook to impose peace in various Italian cities in the 1260s.

18. Cinzio Violante, *La pataria milanese e la riforma ecclesiastica* (Rome, 1955) and his collected essays, *Studi sulla cristianità medioevale*, 2d ed. (Milan, 1975).

19. Antonio Rigon, "Chiesa e vita religiosa à Padova nel duecento," *S. Antonio: 1231–1981, Il suo tempo il suo culto, e la sua città* (Padua, 1981), 284–307, esp. 285.

20. I have recently made this argument in "Economy and Society in the Kingdom of Sicily under Frederick II," delivered at the Conference on Intellectual Life at the Court of Frederick II, Washington, D.C., 18 January 1990, and my *Anatomy of a Crusade* (Philadelphia, 1986), in which I examine the relation of these conflicts to urban and rural violence (67–88). Baronio (*Monasterium*, 107–65) has written very suggestively about the relation between conflict in the *contado* and urban violence. For a more general discussion, see John K. Hyde, "Contemporary Views on Faction and Civil Strife in Thirteenth- and Fourteenth-Century Italy," in *Violence and Civil Disorder*, ed. Lauro Martines (Berkeley, Cal., 1972), 273–307, and Lauro Martines, "Political Violence in the Thirteenth Century," ibid., 331–53. For a comparison with Padua, see Antonio Rigon, "Chiesa e vita religiosa à Padova," 284–307.

21. Duane Osheim, *An Italian Lordship: The Bishopric of Lucca in the Late Middle Ages* (Berkeley, Cal., 1977), 58–85.

22. *Annales brixiensis, MGHSS* 18:815–19.

23. Ibid. 18:815.

24. Baronio, *Monasterium*, 107–65.

25. *Annales brixiensis, MGHSS* 18:815–16. "Et facta est societas Sancti Faustini, et discordia inter eos et milites, et comes Narisius factus est potestas a predicta societate." After contrasting the *societas* and the *milites*, the annals inform us that Count Narisius was elected podestà of the *Societas Sancti Faustini*. The tie to the church of Saint Faustinus is not made clear in the sources, but it is apparent that the significance is both political and religious. Heers, *Parties and Political Life*, 73.

26. Fè d'Ostiani, "Conti rurali," 25.

27. *Annales brixiensis, MGHSS* 18:816; Baronio, *Monasterium*, 95–96.

28. *Annales brixiensis, MGHSS* 18:816; *Annales Placentini Guelfi, MGHSS* 18:423.

29. Odorici, *Storie bresciane* 7:70; Fè d'Ostiani, "Conti rurali," 16–29.

30. Malvezzi, *Chronicon, RISS* 14:907. "milites . . . leones coronatos." Malvezzi may here be noting a more formal group with crowned lions as their symbol. But cf. Baronio, *Monasterium*, 171–76 for the application of the term *leones* to the supporters of the monastery.

31. Guerrini, *Conti di Martinengo*, 103, 107–76.

32. Ibid., 133–40; Fè d'Ostiani, "Conti rurali," 29.

33. Guerrini, *Conti di Martinengo*, 138–40; Odorici, *Storie bresciane* 5:284–97.

34. *Annales brixiensis, MGHSS* 18:817. See also Powell, *Anatomy of a Crusade*, 67–87.

35. *Annales brixiensis, MGHSS* 18:817–18.

36. *LP* 19:598–99.

37. Ibid. 19:600–602. Mattheus described in graphic terms the violence used against him and his men to expel him from Brescia in his testimony before the imperial chancellor, Conrad of Metz: "trahebant lapides super domum ibi erat

et quod servientes eius graviter percusserunt." He was at this time a guest of the bishop. This action, on the site of the future city hall, may explain its location. See Odorici, *Storie bresciane* 5:299–304.

38. The first mention of heresy in conjunction with the political dispute between the *milites* and the supporters of Mattheus of Corregia is found in a letter of Pope Honorius III, written on 11 September 1224, to the "Militibus et populo Brixiensibus," deploring heretical divisions in the city and praising those who supported the efforts of Bishop Albert of Brescia and Bishop William of Modena, whom Honorius had appointed the preceding May to persuade Lombard civil administrations to enforce the statute against heresy promulgated at the Fourth Lateran Council of 1215. Pressutti 2:242 (4960 [4 May 1224]) and Pressutti 2:271 (5114 [11 September 1224]). The appointment of Albert was directly related to the discovery of heresy among supporters of the Brescian *milites*.

39. The problem of heresy has been one of the most vexing in medieval historiography. Even today there is little real consensus on many aspects of it. The most comprehensive account of medieval Catharism is found in Arno Borst, *Die Katharer*, Schriften der Monumenta Germaniae Historica, vol. 12 (Stuttgart, 1953). Walter Wakefield, *Heresy, Crusade, and Inquisition in Southern France, 1100–1250* (London, 1974) is useful for comparative purposes. The best account in English is by Malcolm Lambert, *Medieval Heresy* (London, 1977). For Italy, Gioacchino Volpe, *Movimenti religiosi e sette ereticali nella società medievale italiana* (Florence, 1922) is the classic study. More recent works are Raoul Manselli, *L'eresia del male* (Naples, 1961) and Savino Savini, *Il catarismo italiano ed i suoi vescovi nei secoli xiii e xiv* (Florence, 1958); for Brescia, see Lodovico Muratori, *Antiquitates Italicae medii aevi*, 6 vols. (Milan, 1738–42) 5:90; Odorici, *Storie bresciane* 5:319–20. On the linkage of the heretics with the *milites*, cf. Honorius III's letter of 9 January 1225 to Bishop Albert of Brescia and Bishop Bonaventure of Rimini, *MGH Ep.* 1:189–90.

40. Lambert, *Medieval Heresy,* 115.

41. Ibid., 159.

42. *Die Konstitutionen Friedrichs II* (Cologne, 1973) I:1. Frederick's legislation against heresy speaks of its progress from the North to the South: "adeo quod ab Italiae finibus, praesertim a partibus Lombardiae, in quibus pro certo perpendimus ipsorum nequitiam amplius abundare."

43. Rigon, "Chiesa e vita religiosa à Padova," 293–94.

44. Greenaway, *Arnold of Brescia;* A. Frugoni, *Arnoldo da Brescia nelle fonti del secolo XII* (Rome, 1954); Borst, *Die Katharer,* 88–89.

45. Walter L. Wakefield and Austin P. Evans, *Heresies of the High Middle Ages: Selected Sources Translated and Annotated* (New York, 1969), 149.

46. Ibid., 687.

47. Pressutti 2:242 (4960 [4 May 1224]).

48. Ibid. 2:242 (4960 [4 May 1224]).

49. Ibid. 2:271 (5114 [11 September 1224]).

50. *MGH Ep.* 1:190.

51. "Quia igitur in civitate Brixiae quasi quodam hereticorum domicilio ipsi heretici et eorum fautores nuper in tantam vesaniam proruperunt." Ibid. 1:190. Borst, *Die Katharer,* 104–29; Thomas of Spalato, *Historia, MGHSS* 29:580.

52. Baronio, *Monasterium*, 83–118, provides substantial background. See also Fè d'Ostiani, "Conti rurali," 25–36.

53. Antoine Dondaine, "La hierarchie cathare en Italie," *Archivum fratrum praedicatorum* 20 (1950): 234–324, identifies Lanfranchus de Brixia as Cathar *diaconus* of Bergamo (324).

54. Dondaine, "La hierarchie cathare," 281–88 furnishes ample evidence of the extensive network of heretics in Desenzano. The importance of Desenzano probably sprang in part from its location. Heretics could move easily along the lake and on the roads through the mountains. Wakefield and Evans, *Heresies*, 162, translate the treatise on heretics by Anselm of Alessandria, O.P., edited by Dondaine (cf. note 53). Among those places referred to is Mosio, where an important assembly of the Cathars took place in the late twelfth century (p. 162). See also Savini *Il catarismo italiano*, 97–99; Borst, *Die Katharer*, 236–37. Note esp. Hamund of Casaloldo, ibid., 244–45. On parties, cf. Borst, 254–55, note 3. Merchants also travelled through these towns, which possessed active markets in this period. Ugo Vaglia, "I mercati della Valle Sabbia," *Archivio storico lombardo*, ser. 8, vol. 10 (1960): 116–30.

55. *MGH Ep.* 1:197–98; Volpe, *Movimenti religiosi*, 101–4.

56. *Le Pergamene del monastero di S. Giulia di Brescia, 1043–1590*, Monumenta Brixiensis Historica, vol. 7 (Brescia, 1984), 56, note 174. See also *LP* 19:138, 177, 181, 195, 233. It is not clear if all are our Bonaventura.

57. *MGH Ep.* 1:215–16.

58. Powell, *Anatomy of a Crusade*, 197.

59. On Honorius III's dealings with the nobles of southern France after the Fourth Lateran Council, see ibid., 49, note 31. Cf. also the policies of Innocent III at the council, ibid., 43–44.

60. See above, note 56.

61. *LP* 19:203.

62. *LP* 19:207. See also *LP* 19:294, 371, 385, 401.

63. *LP* 19:300, 677, 952, as well as the *Le Pergamene monastero di S. Giulia*, 64 and 69. On the defense of Montechiari against Frederick by the Ugoni, cf. Alfredo Bosisio, *Storia di Brescia* 1:669, note 1. Raymond de Ugonibus witnessed a transfer of land to the Dominicans in 1227. Ordorici, *Storie bresciane* 7:90.

64. *LP* 19:677. Albertanus is also a witness to this treaty with Bergamo.

65. Ibid. 19:627.

66. Ibid. 19:608.

67. Rigon, "Chiesa e vita religiosa à Padova," 293–94; Borst, *Die Katharer*, 254–55. But see also Giorgio Cracco, "Da commune di famiglie à città satellite," *Storia di Vicenza* (Vicenza, 1988) 2:99–100.

2. *Forma Vitae:* The Transformation of the Senecan Tradition

THE WRITING OF the *De amore et dilectione Dei et proximi et aliarum rerum et de forma vitae* marks a major change in the medieval approach to morality. It stands near the beginning of the development of a new moral science founded on reason and natural law. At the same time, it continues to draw on the rich Senecan tradition that had informed so much of the moral literature of the twelfth century. While previous scholarship has viewed this and other of Albertanus's works largely as a continuation of that tradition into the first half ot the thirteenth century, the present study argues that the *De amore* combines elements of the Senecan tradition with contemporary ideas about religious rules for the laity to create the basis for a new vision of society.[1] The resultant synthesis of Judaeo-Christian and classical moral philosophy is an authentic product of the emerging lay culture of early thirteenth-century Italy. The goal of the *De amore* is the realization of the social aspirations of communal society as a group of citizens freely sworn to uphold a body of rules in pursuit of happiness.

Albertanus dedicated the *De amore* to his son Vincentius. The circumstances under which it was written—Albertanus's capture and imprisonment in Cremona—lend credence to the importance of the personal element in his decision to take up his pen at this time. "With how much love and affection, my fatherly love embraces your filial subjection, I can hardly tell you."[2] Vincent was already a young man, probably eighteen years old or even older. He must have had a good knowledge of Latin, because his father urged him to revise the *De amore,* a task that he could only have undertaken if his education was virtually complete. Moreover, Albertanus emphasized the personal meaning of his treatise to his son: "and when it will give you grace, you will change your life, and so you will conquer [*vinces*] and will flee from vice and sin so that you will be worthy to be called Vincent [that is, the one who conquers]."[3] This father's pun sums up basic attitudes between father and son that are to us strikingly modern. Albertanus wanted his son to be strong in the face of adversity. He wanted him to know how much he loved him, but he was especially concerned that Vincent should hold to those values his father was trying to impart to him in the *De amore*. His treatise was an extension of his role as a father.

But the title of Albertanus's treatise raises the question whether it was merely directed to his son or was intended for a larger audience. Certainly, it was not just the product of the circumstances surrounding his captivity. It was the result of much thought and study, probably over a period of several years.[4] The address to his son did have a special meaning, but was probably not the principal motive for Albertanus's writing. Appropriate though his message was to his own family, it had an even greater meaning to the larger world. When Albertanus told Vincent, "you will change your life," he was summing up the meaning of his treatise for all who would read it. But what kind of change did he have in mind?

In a thesis written at Nanterre in the mid 1970s Hedwige Peemens-Poullet argued that Albertanus was fundamentally a conservative moralist who forged new themes in the service of the dominant class.[5] Albertanus's writing was aimed at supporting the status quo. However, she does note that he had no hostility toward any particular social class, "neither toward the nobility, nor the *petite bourgeoisie,* nor the poor."[6] Such a view hardly does justice to the breadth of Albertanus's concerns or the strength of his protests against the power of the rich.[7] But for Peemens-Poullet, Albertanus's writings were directed solely to the goal of educating his son to be an honest man and ensuring his eternal salvation.[8] She places him firmly within the stoic tradition of Seneca and Cicero, but with his chief purposes influenced by his Christian concern for the world to come rather than the present life. She does not see the *De amore* as promoting any kind of structural change within society.[9] Its message was concerned only with the moral reform of the individual. To be sure, Albertanus's writings are not without interest in the history of medieval education, but, in her view, they have little to offer regarding the development of social or political theory.

This reading of the *De amore,* even if we ignore its other defects, is based on the idea that it was written chiefly to be read by members of a restricted group. In her view, Albertanus did not envisage his work as one to be "diffused" throughout society.[10] Peemens-Poullet suggests that the great popularity of the work, achieved within a short period after its composition, was not intended by its author. But, once diffused, she regards it as a guide for the education of the young. While there is merit to this view, there is also evidence that it only partially explains the nature of the *De amore*.

As we have already suggested, the title of Albertanus's treatise itself raises questions about the motivation behind its writing. The complete title was *De amore et dilectione Dei et proximi et aliarum rerum et de forma vitae*. This rather cumbersome title is essential to understanding the nature of his work. It is not an easy title to translate into English. Both *amor* and *dilectio* mean love. *Amor* signifies love in general, for example, the love of God or parents as well as the selfish love that stems from *eros*. *Dilectio*, on the other hand, has a more restricted meaning. It refers to the human act of loving, to the conscious act of the will that motivates human love. We might speak of *dilectio* as "affection."[11] Albertanus's treatise deals with love in general, and with human "affection" for God, neighbor, and other goods, both material and immaterial. It also concerns the "form of life." The term *forma vitae* is central to our interpretation of the *De amore*. *Forma vitae* is a quasi-technical term that occurs frequently in medieval texts and signifies a way of life under a religious rule.[12] Pope Innocent III used it to refer to the rule he granted to the Humiliati in 1201, a useful example since it involves the confirmation of a rule of a religious community composed of both clerics and laity, both men and women.[13] But this notion of the *De amore* as a rule is also reflected in the opening words of the title, which seem to have been drawn from the rule of Saint Augustine, whose popularity had mushroomed during the twelfth century. The first heading of Augustine's rule is "De charitate Dei et proximi, unione cordium et communitate rerum." The opening words of the rule include the exhortation: "Ante omnia, fratres charissimi, diligatur Deus et proximus."[14] Interestingly, in the thirteenth century there was a copy of the rule of Saint Augustine in the church of San Giovanni de foris in Brescia with the title *Institutiones Sancti Augustini episcopi de vita canonicorum* [The Rule of Saint Augustine on the canonical life]. Immediately following this title are the words, "These are the things that we order to be observed in this rule so that dwelling canonically after the principal precepts, I speak of the love of God and of neighbor" [dillectionem dico Dei et proximi].[15] While we cannot know if Albertanus was familiar with this manuscript, this evidence does show the extent of Augustinian influence on his title and how easily he could have obtained knowledge of the Augustinian rule.

But the original inspiration that shaped Albertanus's thinking most likely came not from Saint Augustine or from any religious rule but from a marginal note in a manuscript of the letters of Seneca to Lucilius.[16] Acting on a suggestion made by Leighton Reynolds, Claudia Villa has studied two important tenth-century manuscripts in the Biblioteca Queriniana in Brescia that contain extensive marginal notes in a thirteenth-century hand.[17] These manuscripts of the *De civitate Dei* of Saint Augustine and the *Epistolae morales ad lucilium* of Lucius Annaeus Seneca. The latter was to be a major source for the writings of Albertanus of Brescia. Villa's aim was to prove that Albertanus had annotated both of these manuscripts in his own hand. To this end, she compared the marginal notes and Albertanus's citations from the *Ad lucilium* with his treatises.[18] She found no evidence to support her argument in the manuscript of Augustine's *De civitate Dei,* but was able to demonstrate that Albertanus had made extensive use of the Seneca manuscript and since the marginal notes in both manuscripts were in the same hand, he had undoubtedly read both. She also showed that his use of the Seneca manuscript had to precede his writing of the *De amore* in 1238.[19] Villa's work is extremely important, therefore, not merely for linking Albertanus to these manuscripts and their marginal notes, but for providing a basis for further study of the intellectual formation of Albertanus of Brescia.

Study of Seneca's sixth letter to his friend Lucilius in the Brescian manuscript provides the basis for a new interpretation of Albertanus's use of the Senecan tradition. In this letter, Seneca begins by announcing that he is "not only being reformed, but transformed."[20] He wants to share this "sudden change" with his friend. He promises to send Lucilius the actual books from which he has learned, having marked certain passages to save time. He advises him:

> Of course, however, the living voice and the intimacy of a common life will help you more than the written word. You must go to the scene of the action, first, because men put more faith in their eyes than in their ears, and second, because the way is long if one follows precepts, but short and helpful if one follows patterns.[21]

He goes on the describe how Cleanthes did not merely listen to the lectures of Zeno, but "shared in his life, saw into his hidden purposes, and watched him to see whether he lived according to his own rules."

The Queriniana manuscript of Seneca's letters has a note in a tenth-century hand, most likely that of the copyist, on the left-hand margin of folio 4v opposite the words "the living voice and the intimacy of the common life will help you more than the written word." So impressed was this early reader by these words that he wrote "de forma vite" just at this point.[22] It seem likely that this reader was himself a monk and was applying the words of Seneca to life under a monastic rule. Albertanus read Seneca's words and saw the marginal note. We know that this letter had a special meaning to him because he not only made several marginal notes, but singled out a sentence from it that he included in the *De amore*: "No good thing is pleasant to possess without friends to share it."[23] The words "de forma vite" provide a link between the concept of a religious rule and the rule of life laid out by Seneca for his friend Lucilius. The first stage in the transformation of the concept of a religious rule to secular use had sprung, in all likelihood, from the pen of some long dead monk-copyist, but it was the decision of Albertanus to include it in the title of his treatise that demonstrates how these words result in a new approach to the Senecan tradition.

The reading of both the *De civitate Dei* and the letters to Lucilius was a formative influence in the shaping of Albertanus's interests and ideas. Although Villa has noted that it is not possible to trace direct citations from the *De civitate Dei* to Albertanus's writings, it is quite easy, once we recognize Albertanus's marginalia, to see which passages in Augustine attracted his interest. For example, he made a note of the following passage from Book Four: "No one doubts that it is easy to find a man who shrinks from becoming a king, but no one can be found who does not wish to be happy."[24] Such a strong statement about the human desire for happiness agreed totally with his ideas and reinforced his reading of Seneca. He also singled out the story of Lucius Valerius and Quintius Cincinnatus, used by Augustine as examples of pagan Romans who cared little for the goods of this world.[25] In the margin, Albertanus wrote "On the poverty of Lucius Valerius" and "On the poverty of Quintius Cincinnatus." Saint Augustine had pointed them out as examples so that Christians who practiced voluntary poverty would not believe that they were superior in all ways to the ancient Romans. Albertanus does not mention either Valerius or Cincinnatus in his writings, but his interest in the problem of poverty was profound and complex and it is therefore not surprising that this passage should have attracted his attention.[26]

Villa has found numerous passages in which Albertanus's reading of the letters of Seneca resulted in direct quotations in his writings. She has also been able to demonstrate that some of these come from the Brescian manuscript.[27] Additional examples could easily be produced, but one will suffice. On folio 77v of the Brescian manuscript of Seneca's letters,

Albertanus wrote "Nota sermo cum vita concordet [Note that speech should harmonize with life]."[28] At this point, he was reading a text of Seneca, which, because of its importance, will be quoted in both Latin and English:

> Haec sit propositi nostri summa, quod sentimus loquamur, quod loquimur sentiamus; concordet sermo cum vita.

> [Let this be the heart of our rule: let us say what we feel and feel what we say; let speech harmonize with life.][29]

Albertanus quoted this passage in the *De amore*. It suited his purpose perfectly, for the Latin word *propositum,* used by Seneca, referred in the Middle Ages to a religious rule. Moreover, in another place, although he had not made a marginal note, he quotes the following passage from Seneca: "Vita sine proposito vaga est [Life without a rule is aimless]."[30] Villa was concerned chiefly to prove Albertanus's authorship of marginal notes found in these manuscripts. She did not attempt to show how his study influenced his thought. These examples illustrate that the Senecan manuscript played a critical role in Albertanus's conception of the *De amore* as a rule of life.

The notion of a rule that would transform the lives of individuals was deeply rooted in Christianity, particularly in monasticism.[31] From a starting point in key Gospel passages that came to denote a special way of imitating the life of Christ, to the composition of the great monastic rules of antiquity, the notion of transformation of the individual through submission to a rule flourished in Christian thought. After the fourth century, there was increased recognition that this transformation was most effective for the greatest number of those dwelling within a communitarian, or cenobitical, structure. During the ninth and tenth centuries, the triumph of the Benedictine Rule in Western monasticism established a norm for the relationship between individual and community that would eventually have an impact on social and political ideas.[32] That process was encouraged by the growth of the monastic, papal, and popular reform movements of the eleventh and twelfth centuries, which witnessed the proliferation of new forms of religious life among both the clergy and the laity. Not only were ancient eremitical forms revived by the Carthusian and the Camaldolese monks, but new religious orders sprang into existence, drawing inspiration directly from the Gospels and motivated by an intense desire to live according to the standards of the apostolic life, with special emphasis on voluntary poverty. Among the most notable were the Premonstratensians, founded by Norbert of Xanten, and the Order of Grandmont, with its radical rejection of property, founded by Stephen of Muret.

At the same time, there was a veritable explosion of new groups for both clergy and laity such as the Humiliati, who were especially popular in the cities of Lombardy but were suspected by many of heresy. Even some former Waldensian heretics obtained recognition of their rule. Numerous confraternities sprang up in even the smaller towns. Larger towns and cities often had several, including quasi-religious associations organized by members of the medical and legal professions.[33] Albertanus himself was a member of such an association in Brescia. At every level, among both clergy and laity, late twelfth-century society was caught up in a yearning for rules that seemed insatiable. At the Fourth Lateran Council in 1215, the decision was taken to prohibit the proliferation of new religious rules, requiring that those desiring to form new religious institutions must accept an existing rule.[34] But, as Giles Constable has recently observed, this prohibition met with little success. He cites Goscelin of Saint Bertin to make his point: "The palm of Christ is denied to no sex, no age, no condition."[35] Goscelin reflected accurately the attitudes of his contemporaries concerning the religious life. Men and women, clerics and laity, rich and poor, all sought the havens offered by religious rules. Recent historiography has shown the socioreligious rationale behind this development, particularly as a shelter against poverty or to ensure prayers after death.[36] But the desire for rules also reflected a deep-seated insecurity that sprang from the divisive tensions and fragmented factionalism of this society. These are the concerns best demonstrated in the *De amore*.

Albertanus combined the powerful symbol of the religious rule with the classical moralist tradition, chiefly—though not exclusively—through his study of the letters of Seneca. A study of his use of the concept of *propositum* (rule), confirms that its classical and Christian meanings had been fused in his thinking. Nor was this adaptation merely a matter of "baptizing" Seneca in the way that modern scholarship has often spoken of the "baptism" of Aristotle.[37] Albertanus's marginal notes show that he understood that Seneca's paganism was at odds with his own Christianity, especially on the issue of suicide.[38] In spite of his reservations, he recognized that Seneca's effort to provide guidance to his friend Lucilius was a valuable source of wisdom for the rule that he was developing to meet the needs of human society as whole. To him, Seneca, like Cicero and even the Hebrew Wisdom literature, was a voice of reason. Albertanus was not writing a religious rule. In his hands, the notion of rule took on a broader social meaning. Rather than a body of legislation to guide the quest of elite, dedicated, religious souls toward spiritual transformation, Albertanus's rule was a means whereby ordinary human beings could transform themselves. The *vita monastica* had become a model for all human society.

Albertanus frequently cites Seneca's use of the concept of *propositum*, or rule, in the *De amore*, but he draws from other authors as well.[39] He quotes the *Sententiae* by popular Roman author Publilius Syrus (first century B.C.): "He is more seriously angered who acts against the rule [*propositum*]."[40] He also quotes passages from Ovid and Cicero in which this idea occurs.[41] Throughout, he shows his preference for this language, as when he attributes the following quotation to Cassiodorus, himself author of a famous rule: "Nobis propositum est Deo iuvante sic vincere ut subjecti se doleant nostrum dominium tardius acquisisse."[42] *Propositum* as used here embodies the notion of rule over a subjected people in such a way that those who have been overcome regret that they were not conquered earlier. In every instance where the term *propositum* is used in the *De amore*, it receives a positive value. This was not accidental. On two occasions, he cites the following sentence from the *Moralium dogma philosophorum*: "Constantia est stabilitas animi firma et in proposito perseverans [Constancy is a firm stability of mind and a persevering in a rule]."[43] The significance of this quotation within the context of the present discussion is immediately evident. The monastic context of this definition is present in the words "stability" and "persevering," attributes that were paramount in the monastic vocation. But Albertanus applies them to society as a whole. Earlier in the *De amore*, he has paraphrased this same quotation: "Constantia est stabilitas animi firma et in *bono* proposito perseverans."[44] The addition of *bonum* (good) to the word for rule confirms our interpretation of his use of *propositum*. "Persevering in a good rule" shows how he attaches a positive meaning to *propositum* in order to make clear the meaning of his treatise as a rule of life.

The remainder of this chapter will explore the sources and structure of the *De amore* in order to show its relationship to other genres and to pursue further the debt that Albertanus owed to various religious rules. But our purpose will not be merely to identify sources but to demonstrate the kind of interaction that occurred between Albertanus and the works he used.

In order to understand the degree to which the approach taken by Albertanus transformed the Senecan tradition, we need to explore the nature of that tradition in the early Middle Ages.[45] During the patristic age, Seneca was one of a small number of pagan moralists, chiefly Stoics, who enjoyed a high reputation among Christian writers. (Another was Cicero, whom we will examine below.) Seneca came to be regarded in some circles as a crypto-Christian. Indeed, it was thought that he had carried on a correspondence with Saint Paul. There is, however, no indication that Albertanus was aware of this tradition or had access to the spurious correspondence between the apostle and the philosopher.[46] On the other hand, he did know and used extensively Archbishop Martin of Braga's (d. A.D. 580) *Formula honestae vitae*, which from the twelfth century had circulated as a "genuine" work by Seneca under the title *De quattuor virtutibus cardinalibus* [On the Four Cardinal Virtues].[47] In fact, it is highly likely that Martin's work was an epitome of a lost work of Seneca. More pertinent to our purposes, it was an example of the genre known as a "mirror for princes," a work written specifically to instruct a potential or actual ruler on the virtues proper to his office. Thus, it had already, as its title indicates, something of the character of a rule, though not in any specific sense. Seneca enjoyed considerable prestige in the twelfth century, as we may see from the writings of Petrus Alfonsi (1062–1110?), the author of the *Disciplina clericalis,* and William of Conches (1080–ca. 1150), to whom the *Moralium dogma philosophorum* has been attributed. To these we might easily add others, including the poems of Walter of Chatillon (ca. 1135–after 1184).[48] Peter Abelard, who had a particular interest in moral science, referred to Seneca as "the most edifying of all the moral philosophers."[49] In the century prior to the translation of Aristotle's political and ethical treatises, Seneca was probably the most important source of classical moral philosophy.

Not all twelfth-century moral writers, however, found their sources in the writings of the Stoic philosophers. The *De amicitia* of the letter-writer and humanist Peter of Blois, for example, emphasized a theological approach to friendship, derived from a Cistercian source and culminating in love of the Holy Trinity. Charity for Peter was based on the theological concept of the communion of the saints.[50] Albertanus does not seem to have drawn on such theological discussions of love and friendship, but found his inspiration in writers who employed the reason of the ancients as a foundation for their own. His attitude toward authority was based on his great respect for the wisdom of ancient writers, but he does not accord them a status greater than the wise men of his own time.[51] His views were not markedly different from those of Thomas Aquinas writing later in the

thirteenth century. For Thomas, the Hebrew Wisdom literature represented the theological philosophy of the Jews, while the ethical writings
of the Romans were founded on a moral science.[52] Albertanus saw in all of
these sources a wisdom based upon reason rather than divine revelation.
Man could only understand how to act properly after a profound examination of all the factors and circumstances involved in an action.

The major twelfth-century sources that shaped the thought of Albertanus were of French origin or were particularly popular in France.[53]
French influence is evident in all of Albertanus's works, including the *De
amore*. His classicism owed much to that of the French schools. The same
was true of his reading of his contemporaries. Albertanus was certainly
familiar with the literature of courtly love, at least through the writings of
Andreas Capellanus, whom he quoted in the *De amore* on more than a
dozen occasions.[54] He also quoted widely from one of Andreas's principle
sources, the Roman poet Ovid.[55] Andreas wrote a scholastic treatise on
courtly love about 1186 in which he exposed both its positive values and its
shortcomings.[56] Albertanus on the other hand used Andreas chiefly to provide discussion of particular kinds of human relationships, and most often
disapproved of his views.

This approach contrasted with his use of the writings of Petrus Alfonsi, mentioned above, a layman and a convert from Judaism, whose *Disciplina clericalis* was one of the most popular collections of moral tales,
many drawn from eastern sources, in the late twelfth and early thirteenth
centuries.[57] Petrus exemplified the kind of practical morality that appealed
to Albertanus, who had no apparent interest in the tales with which Petrus
illustrated his moral teachings. Albertanus cited him to bolster his moral
arguments, but he was much more concerned about the theoretical structure of his own treatise than about the *exempla* in which Petrus's work
abounded. Indeed, it was most probably its logical organization that attracted Albertanus to the *Moralium dogma philosophorum*, which was an
early product of the twelfth-century French schools.[58]

Written before mid century and dedicated in all probability to the
young Henry II prior to his accession to the English throne in 1154, the
Moralium was a model scholastic treatise.[59] Many of the topics treated
closely parallel those discussed by Albertanus in his own writings. Opening with a chapter on deliberation in the giving of counsel, it proceeds to
a discussion of honesty—with subheadings for prudence, justice, injustice,
fortitude, and temperance—each with further subdivisions.[60] Following
its treatment of honesty, it moves to a comparison of honest men and of

those things that are useful to human beings. It speaks of material and immaterial goods.[61] Under the latter, it treats wealth in its various forms. Aside from numerous citations that demonstrate the profound debt that Albertanus owed to the *Moralium* for specific moral arguments, it is apparent that he was also inspired by its organization. One example is evident in his discussion of prudence. After stating that prudence is treated under six species, he proceeds to quote a passage from the *Moralium* that discusses the various aspects of prudence.[62] But the most important influence of the *Moralium* is evident in the sections dealing with material and immaterial goods.[63] The scholastic structure of the *De amore* provides further evidence of Albertanus's effort to systematize his treatment of morality. In this way, as in his approach to societal change through his concept of the transforming character of rules, he had moved beyond the Senecan tradition even as it was developed in the *Moralium*.

It is quite clear from his sermons that Albertanus was also familiar with the rules of *proposita* of professional lay confraternities.[64] Through a reading of all of his writings, it is evident that his knowledge extended well beyond these rules to include the rules of the Orders of Penance, which were so popular at this time, and perhaps those of the Humiliati.[65] But the rules of these lay communities were hardly suitable to his purpose, which was aimed at the reform of society. The *proposita* reflect strong clerical influence in the manner in which they seek to protect members from heresy and in their encouragement of liturgical and devotional practices.[66] At the same time, most give evidence of basic tenets that were deeply held by the laity and perhaps also by members of the lower clergy. The sermons delivered by Albertanus to his confrères in Genoa and Brescia show that he was quite familiar with the rules of professional confraternities and often in agreement with them.[67] But they had virtually no impact on the writing of the *De amore* or, indeed, his other treatises. The matter was somewhat different with respect to the rules of the Orders of Penance and the Humiliati. As we read the *De amore*, it becomes clear that Albertanus did not merely leave out provisions that were included in these rules, but differed from them on critical matters. One such area involved the bearing of arms.[68] Virtually all rules of the Orders of Penance, with the exception of groups such as the *Militia Jesu Christi*, founded for members of the knightly class in 1235 by Bartholomew of Vicenza, contained prohibitions on the bearing of arms.[69] Such statutes, which opposed military service by their members, were the cause of conflict with communal authorities throughout northern Italy.[70] Albertanus opposed these statutes, defending the concept of just war and the use of suitable weapons in self-defense.[71] In so doing, he demonstrated the priority of his commitment to communal values rather than to those embodied in the rules of the Orders of Penance.

His position is even clearer if we examine his views on such matters as oaths, food, and clothing.[72] Many rules contained a prohibition against oaths.[73] Opposition to such oaths was not merely theoretical, despite the appeal to the Bible. Oaths were commonly used in forming political groups, which were often seen as oppressive violators of good order.[74] Rejection of oaths was to some degree, therefore, an expression of opposition to the communes and to the conflicts that accompanied their formation. Albertanus opposed these conflicts, but he supported the swearing of oaths. He argued that heretics opposed the taking of oaths, ignoring the existence of opposition to oaths in orthodox rules of penance. His position was based not on religious teaching but on his political commitment to the commune. With this as background, it is easier to understand that Albertanus did not follow the rules of the Orders of Penance in the matter of food and clothing. In particular, he rejected entirely the sumptuary legislation directed against women commonly found in such rules and substituted for it a rule of moderation in both food and dress without specification of gender.[75] From this perspective, it is evident that he used his knowledge of religious rules chiefly as a basis for reacting against particular statutes. He was not writing for those religious persons who desired to dedicate themselves to the *imitatio Christi*, but for those like his sons who lived within the structures of a larger society and whose needs and goals could not be encompassed within the rule of any confraternity.

But what of the argument that Albertanus was primarily a man of law? As we have seen, Aldo Checchini and others have long maintained that the Bolognese rhetorical and legal tradition was important in shaping Albertanus's thought.[76] Reserving discussion of Albertanus's views on rhetoric to the next chapter (on the *De doctrina dicendi et tacendi*), we need to point out here that there is no direct evidence supporting Bolognese influences on the *De amore*.[77] Albertanus's study of law poses difficult problems, as we have already seen. His citations from legal sources, ranging from the *Decretum* of the canonist Gratian to the *Digest* and *Codex* of Justinian, are not numerous.[78] Although there can be no question about his familiarity with the law—hardly surprising for one engaged in his profession—he was not really interested in building a legal foundation to support his views on the nature and reform of society. The twelfth and thirteenth centuries produced a rich body of legal and political literature that contributed substantially to the development of political thought.[79] Some of this, like lawyers' commentaries and glosses, gained importance within the development of the legal profession.[80] Other work such as the podestà literature was the product of increasingly professionalized administrators.[81] By mid century, the new Aristotelian translations began to have an impact on the schools and soon thereafter among the professionals.[82] The emergence of the pre-humanists in the late thirteenth and early fourteenth centuries, men like Albertino Mussato, Giovanni da Nono, and Geremia da Montagnone, belongs to this briefly sketched process.

Albertanus not only reflects an older tradition, one that was drawing to a close in its twelfth-century form to emerge in new ways in the later thirteenth and fourteenth centuries, but he also illustrates early tendencies toward a more structured theory of society based on a moral science. His failure to develop his ideas within a legal framework may be a product of his culture and education, which seem rather distant from the schools of law, but it probably also helps to account for much of his originality. At the same time, there can be little doubt that his strong ties to the twelfth century had a critical effect on his place in Italian and European social thought.

It would be a mistake, however, to see Albertanus's influence in his own time from the limited perspectives offered by hindsight. By placing the *De amore* in the context of its own age, viewing it as a rule of life for society, we can arrive at a better understanding of its meaning. Its approach to fundamental societal change is evident from Albertanus's definition of society: "This is society, I say, in which all things that men consider worthy of pursuit are present: honor, glory, peace, and joy; when these are present there is happiness."[83] The source for this definition of society as the pursuit of happiness is of course Seneca. The term *beata vita* (happiness) used by Albertanus in this quote is taken directly from that author. It does not reflect an aspiration for eternal life as some have suggested, though Albertanus certainly entertained such desires and expressed them elsewhere.[84] His definition of society expressed the actual purpose of the *De amore* as a rule. He was looking for a means to achieve change. He saw the moral transformation of the individual as the agency of that change.

The idea of a rule as a means for achieving change was, as we have seen, totally familiar within the context of Christian thought. But its application to society as a whole was, so far as I am aware, unique to Albertanus of Brescia. Only he saw the concept of a religious rule as a potent symbol for societal change. Not surprisingly, he chose to end his treatise by discussing conversion to the Lord.[85] The historical link between rule and conversion was very close and was widely understood among the educated in medieval society. Conversion was a free act. The symbolism of freedom and submission to a rule had a particular meaning to the world of the communes, those freely sworn associations bound by statutes. In the *De amore*, therefore, we find an example of the medieval capacity to transform the sacred into the secular in the quest for a better society. Moreover, in this instance Albertanus was beginning to explore concepts that underlay social mores and law. He was applying the wisdom of past and present to an understanding of human behavior. For this reason the *De amore* deserves special recognition in the study of the medieval pursuit of happiness.

Notes

1. There is no recent study of the *De amore* save that found in Marta Ferrari, based on earlier writings by Aldo Checchini and Thor Sundby, which contain rather brief discussions. Ferrari, "Intorno ad alcuni sermoni inediti di Albertano da Brescia," *Atti del istituto veneto di scienze, lettere ed arti* 109 (1950–51): 79–80; Checchini, "Un guidice del secolo decimoterzo: Albertano da Brescia," *Atti del reale istituto veneto di scienze, lettere ed arti* 79:2 (1911–12): 1423–95; Sundby, *Liber consolationis et consilii* (Copenhagen, 1873), vii. Claudia Villa, "La tradizione della 'Ad Lucilium' e la cultura di Brescia dall'età carolingia ad Albertano," *Italia medioevale e umanistica* 12 (1969): 9–51, also has some interesting references, discussed later in this chapter. Sharon Hiltz's transcription of the *De amore* from the Pennsylvania manuscript in her dissertation is the only modern edition. Hiltz, "*De amore et dilectione Dei et proximi et aliarum rerum et de forma vita:* An Edition" (Ph.D. dissertation, University of Pennsylvania, 1980). Her dissertation also contains a brief introduction, ix–xvi.

2. Hiltz, "*De amore*," 1. "Quanto amore quantaque dilectione mea paterna caritas tuam diligat filialem subiectionem, vix tibi possem narrare, vel lingua mea posset aliquatenus explicari." All translations are mine unless otherwise noted.

3. Ibid., 289. "Hec tibi, fili karissime, de amore et dilectione Dei et proximi et aliarum rerum et de forma vite breviter et summatim scribere curavi, non tamen ad plenum propter parvitatem mee scientie. Verum quia ut ait lex, 'Qui non subtiliter factum tantum dat laudabilior est quam primus invenit.' Tu invocato Dei omnipotentis nomine ex ingenio ab eo tibi prestito hoc opusculum emendabis et augere studebis, et cum dederit tibi gratiam vitam mutabis, et vitia et peccata ita *vinces*, atque fugabis, *ut merito Vincentius valeas nuncupari*. Viriliter ergo age

confortetur cor tuum et sustine Dominum et ad regnum celorum satage pervenire. Ad quod ille nos conducat qui sine fine vivit et regnat. Amen." (Italics mine.)

4. Albertanus was captured on 26 August 1238, and released about October 6. Even if we stretch these dates a bit to accommodate delays, we are left with the fact that five or six weeks was much too short a period for both the research and writing of the *De amore*. Moreover, Villa's proof that Albertanus used the Brescia, Queriniana, manuscript of Seneca's letters (B II 6) to Lucilius in preparing the *De amore* (Villa, "Tradizione," 28–34), makes it clear that Albertanus was engaged in his studies for a very considerable period. My own study of this manuscript and of the manuscript of Augustine's *De civitate Dei* (Brescia, Queriniana, G III 3), also annotated by Albertanus, suggests that he read the Senecan manuscript at least twice, since there is evidence of later annotation in his hand. See Queriniana, B II 6, fol. 103v, where the marginal notes are partly in black and partly in red ink. On fol. 14v, the red ink partially covers the black, showing that the notes in red were made later. These notes are much fewer in number and suggest more a review than a thorough restudy of the manuscript. On the other hand, the Augustine manuscript was annotated entirely in black. As a hypothesis, I suggest that Albertanus read the *Epistolae morales ad lucilium* first, then the *City of God*, but at almost the same time. The marginal note (Queriniana, G III 3, fol. 36r), "non textum Senecae," which is opposite Augustine's remark in Book 5, 8, 12–13, "Annaei Senecae sunt, nisi fallor, hi versus," suggests that Albertanus was already familiar with Seneca when he read this part of the *De civitate Dei*. (N.B. The references to the *De civitate Dei* are to the Corpus Christianorum edition.) After this initial reading, he reviewed the letters of Seneca. Villa's research seems to prove, on the basis of textual similarities, that Albertanus either took accurate notes from this manuscript or that he had it in his possession at the time he wrote the *De amore*.

5. Hedwige Peemans-Poullet, "Principes, pédagogues, et classes sociales au XIIIe siècle," 2 vols. (Thése de 3eme cycle, Paris X–Nanterre, 1975) 2:28. See also *Letteratura italiana. Il letterato e le istituzione,* ed. A. A. Rosa (Turin, 1982) I:660–62.

6. Peemans-Poullet, "Principes" 2:32.

7. Albertanus's attitude toward the powerful was strongly influenced by his view that there was little that could be done to control their excesses. This view is expressed in the *Liber Consolationis*. Sundby, *Liber,* 78; cf. also Hiltz, "*De amore,*" 76, 87. "Potentioribus enim pares esse non possumus" (Hiltz, "*De amore,*" 76). He strongly opposed their abuse of power, however, as is evident from a passage in his second sermon: "et liberare debemus pro posse pauperes a potentibus" (*Sermones quattuor,* 30–31).

8. Peemans-Poullet, "Principes" 2:84.

9. Ibid. 2:32.

10. Ibid. 2:27.

11. I would like to thank Giles Constable for this suggestion.

12. See note 22.

13. Meersseman, *Dossier,* 282, 290.

14. "Regula S. Augustini," *PL* 32:1377.

15. Cosimo D. Fonseca, *Medioevo canonicale* (Milan, 1970), 112–13, and Table IX, which reproduces fol. 2r of MS. Bologna, Bibliotheca Universitaria 2535.

16. Brescia, Queriniana, B II 6, fol. 4v.

17. Leighton D. Reynolds, *The Medieval Tradition of Seneca's Letters* (London, 1965) 100; Villa, "Tradizione," 28–34.

18. Reynolds, *Medieval Tradition*, 100; see note 4 above.

19. Villa, "Tradizione" 28–34. See especially the example reproduced on page 29.

20. Seneca, *Epistulae*, 6. All translations from Seneca are from the Loeb edition.

21. Ibid. 6:5–6. "Plus tamen tibi et viva vox et convictus quam oratio proderit. In rem presentem venias oportet, primum, homines amplius oculis quam auribus credunt; deinde, quia longum iter est per praecepta, breve et efficax per exempla. Zenonem Cleanthes non expressisset, si tantummodo audisset; vitae eius interfuit, secreta perspexit, observavit illum, an ex formula sua viveret."

22. Brescia, Queriniana, B II 6, fol. 4v. See frontispiece.

23. Ibid. "Et alibi, 'Nullius boni sine socio iocunda possessio est'" Hiltz, "*De amore*," 285.

24. Brescia, Queriniana, G III 3, fol. 31r, *De civitate Dei*, 5, 23, 68–69.

25. Brescia, Queriniana, G III 3, fol. 40r, *De civitate Dei*, 5, 18, 97–107.

26. For a discussion of Albertanus's views on wealth and poverty, see Hans Baron, "Franciscan Poverty and Civic Wealth as Factors in the Rise of Humanistic Thought," *Speculum* 13 (1938): 1–37, esp. 3. See also Lester Little, *Religious Poverty and the Profit Economy in Medieval Europe* (Ithaca, 1978) 173–217. But Little does not discuss Albertanus. For Albertanus's attitude toward poverty, see Sundby, *Liber*, 97–99, where he sets forth a positive view of riches. He also presents a negative view of poverty in the *De amore* (Hiltz, "*De amore*," 258–59). However, his sermons reflect not merely a positive attitude toward charity for the poor, but a championing of their cause (*Sermones quattuor*, 19–20). This does not mean that he rejects his earlier position, which is found in his first sermon (*Sermones quattuor*, 14–15). Rather, his discussions show how complex the poverty issue was at this time.

27. Villa "Tradizione," 28–34.

28. Brescia, Queriniana, B II 6, fol. 77v. See Hiltz, "*De amore*," 17.

29. Seneca, *Epistulae*, 74, 4.

30. Hiltz, "*De amore*," 25. Seneca, *Epistulae*, 95, 46.

31. There is an excellent introduction to these matters in C. H. Lawrence, *Medieval Monasticism*, 2d ed. (London, 1990). On the transforming impact of rules, see for example page 28.

32. Ibid., 125–220.

33. Gennaro M. Monti, *Le confraternite medievali dell'alta e media Italia*, 2 vols. (Venice, 1927) 1:5–7; Christopher Black, *Italian Confraternities in the Sixteenth Century* (Cambridge, 1989), 3–5. See also the remarks in Lester Little, *Liberty, Charity, Fraternity: Lay Religious Confraternities at Bergamo in the Age of the Commune* (Bergamo, 1988), 84–92.

34. On the participation of Albertanus, see Chapter 5 as well as *Ordo Fraternitatis* 3:1273–89. On Lateran IV, see *Conciliorum oecumenicorum decreta* (Bologna, 1973), 242, and James M. Powell "The Papacy and the Early Franciscans," *Franciscan Studies* 36 (1976): 248–62.

35. Giles Constable, "The Diversity of Religious Life and the Acceptance of Social Pluralism in the Twelfth Century," *History, Society and the Churches: Essays in Honour of Owen Chadwick*, ed. Derek Beales and Geoffrey Best (Cambridge, 1985), 29–41, deals specifically with the proliferation of religious rules.

36. James R. Banker, *Death in the Community: Memorialization and Confraternities in an Italian Commune in the Late Middle Ages* (Athens, Ga., 1988), 1–14. See above, note 33.

37. Brian Tierney, *Religion, Law and the Growth of Constitutional Thought, 1150–1650*, (Cambridge, 1983), 29.

38. Brescia, Queriniana, B II 6, fol. 68r. In the margin of Seneca's letter 70, 14, which contains a strong defense of suicide, Albertanus writes "Nemo debet fieri sui ipsius homicida." The thought is hardly surprising, but shows that Albertanus was a critical reader.

39. See above, notes 29 and 30.

40. Publilius Syrus, *Sententiae*, (Leipzig, 1880), 153. Albertanus refers this citation to Cassiodorus: "Gravius irascitur qui contra propositum commovetur." Hiltz, "De amore," 76.

41. See for example his citation from Ovid's *Remedia Amoris* in the *De amore* (Hiltz, "De amore," 53). "Utile propositum est sevas extinguere flammas; nec servum vitii pectus habere tuum" (Loeb ed., 180). He also quotes Cicero, who, in this instance, uses the word *regula* for rule instead of *propositum*: "In hiis autem ipsis mediocritas regula optima est" (Hiltz, "De amore," 184).

42. Hiltz, "De amore," 229.

43. Ibid. 268; *Das Moralium Dogma Philosophorum de Guillaume de Conches*, ed. John Holmberg (Uppsala, 1929), 30.

44. Hiltz, "De amore," 265; *Moralium*, 30. (Italics mine.)

45. Reynolds, *Medieval Tradition*, 112; Gérard G. Meersseman, "Seneca, maestro di spiritualità nei suoi opuscoli apocrifi dal XII al XV secolo," *Italia medioevale e umanistica* 16 (1973): 43–133, esp. 45–46.

46. Reynolds, *Medieval Tradition*, 112.

47. Ibid., 112. See also Martin, Archbishop of Braga, *Opera*, ed. Claude Barlow (New Haven, 1950), 204–50.

48. Walter of Chatillon, *Moralisch-satirische Gedichte Walters von Chatillon*, Ed. Karl Strecker (Heidelberg, 1929). Walter, however, is not cited in the *De amore* so far as I can tell.

49. Reynolds, *Medieval Tradition*, 113.

50. Peter of Blois, *De amicitia et de caritate Dei et proximi*, PL 207: 871–958.

51. Hiltz, "De amore," "Introduction," xii-xiv.

52. Karl Morrison, *The Mimetic Tradition of Reform in the West* (Princeton, 1972), 181.

53. Reynolds, *Medieval Tradition*, 104.

54. Hiltz, "*De amore*," 326. Andrè le Chapelain, *Traité de l'amour courtois*, trans. Claude Buridant (Paris, 1974), 7–42.

55. Hiltz, "*De amore*," 333.

56. André le Chapelain, *Traité*, 7–42.

57. Petrus Alfonsi, *The Disciplina Clericalis of Petrus Alfonsi* (Berkeley, Cal., 1977), 3–99. Albertanus also cites the *Liber Kalilae et Dimnae*, which is available today in the version edited by Raymond de Biterris in Léopold Hervieux, *Les Fabulistes Latins depuis le siècle d'Auguste à la fin du moyen age*, 5 vols. (Paris, 1893–99) 5:379–775.

58. *Moralium*, 7–11.

59. Ibid., 6–7.

60. Ibid., 3–4.

61. Ibid.

62. Hiltz, "*De amore*," 269; *Moralium*, 9–11.

63. See especially the sections of the *Moralium* treating *constantia* and other abstract attributes under "alia res." *Moralium*, 4.

64. "Fratres mei, more solito hic congregati, propositum nostre congregationis inspiciamus, circa illud aliqua utilia pertractantes. Propositum certe nostre congregationis triplicem habet causam." *Sermones quattuor*, 3.

65. See for example his second sermon, dealing with poverty and service to the poor. Ibid., 19–34.

66. See Meersseman, *Dossier*, 94–95, 293; Little, *Liberty*, 285.

67. *Sermone inedito di Albertano, guidice di Brescia*, ed. Luigi F. Fè d'Ostiani (Brescia, 1874), 41: "ad nostrum bonum propositum trahere debemus." Also Hiltz, "*De Amore*," 265: "Constancia vero, ut et ita dicetur, est stabilitas animi firma, et in bono proposito perseverans." See also *Sermones quattuor*, 3, 57. In Sermon Four, he refers to the rule as a *lex*.

68. *Sermone inedito*, 35. Also Hiltz, "*De amore*," 207.

69. Meersseman, *Dossier*, 41, 89, 101. See also page 293 on the *Militia Jesu Christi*. Milva Laurenti, "Violenza, guerra, pena di morte: le proposte degli eretici medievali," *Rivista di Storia della chiesa in Italia* 43 (1989): 123–31.

70. John R. H. Moorman, *A History of the Franciscan Order from Its Origins to the Year 1517* (Oxford, 1968), 126.

71. Hiltz, "*De amore*," 207–15.

72. For examples of restrictions on women's dress and ornament, see Meersseman, *Dossier*, 94–95, 106, 110. Hiltz, "*De amore*," 158–60.

73. Little, *Liberty*, 216; Hiltz, "*De amore*," 220–21.

74. On the relationship of oaths, heresy, and judging, see Hiltz, "*De amore*," 222–23.

75. On food, see *Sermones quattuor*, 13. On moderation in speech, ibid., 41. On execess in modesty, see Hiltz, "*De amore*," 277, and 158–60 on moderation.

76. Checchini, *Un guidice*, 1428–43; Ferrari, "Intorno," 75–82.

77. As already noted in the introduction, references to Albertanus's life and activities are rare. While it is certainly true, as Checchini argued, that Albertanus was familiar with the rhetorical tradition, it is interesting to note that he made no use of the *De amicitia* of the Bolognese rhetorician Boncompagna da Signa, a work

he would almost certainly have known if he had studied at Bologna and one which reflected his own interests quite closely. Boncompagno da Signa, *Amicitia,* ed. Sarina Nathan (Rome, 1909).

78. Hiltz, "*De amore,*" 329–30.

79. Tierney, *Religion,* 1–28.

80. Ibid.

81. Joannes de Viterbo, *Liber de regimine civitatum,* ed. G. Salvemini. *Biblioteca Iuridica Medii Aevi,* ed. A. Gaudenzi, vol. 3 (Bologna, 1901) 3:217–71. See also the "Oculus Pastoralis," Muratori, *Antiquitates* 4:95–128.

82. Tierney, *Religion,* 29–30.

83. Hiltz, "*De amore,*" 102: "Hec est, inquam, societas, in qua omnia sunt que putant homines expetenda: honestas, gloria, tranquillitas, atque iocunditas; ut cum hec adsint, beata vita sit, cum sine hiis esse non possint, quod cum optimum maximumque sit." Vatican City, BAV, Vat. Lat. 991:om. cum.

84. Ibid., 289; *Sermones quattuor,* 64.

85. Hiltz, "*De amore,*" 281–86. See also Albertanus's last chapter of the "*De amore*" on the active and contemplative life, 286–89.

3. Language and Power: The Role of Professionalism in Social Change

IN THE *De amore*, Albertanus of Brescia set forth a plan for human happiness that touched the risks of an ordinary life in the world of the communes. He built this plan on the capacity of the individual to achieve a new moral identity through reform, but he went beyond the concentration on change in the individual that characterized his sources by introducing the concept of religious rule as an instrument of societal change. In so doing, Albertanus demonstrated his capacity to work creatively in the still largely unexplored territory of social thought without the guidance of Aristotle, which would prove to be of critical value in the development of social and political theory in the second half of the thirteenth century.

By itself, the *De amore* establishes the claim of Albertanus to be taken seriously in the history of medieval social theory. It removes him from the ranks of moralists and pre-humanists and demonstrates his importance in the transition to synthetic approaches to social theory. More importantly, the *De amore* provides additional evidence for the free-standing nature of medieval political and social thought in relation to past authorities, placing the question of classical influences into a clearer framework than had previously been possible. At the risk of oversimplification, we need only to consider the fortuitous juxtaposition of *forma vitae* and Seneca's sixth letter to Lucilius for insight into the manner in which Albertanus read the letters of the Roman philosopher. This approach provides an interesting key to understanding the medieval imagination.

But the *De amore* was only a first stage in Albertanus's work. Although it established a broad plan, it left unclear the ways in which this plan was to be implemented. The temptation to provide a schematic response is great when we look at the remainder of his writings in light of the new interpretation of the *De amore* presented here. But we need to keep in mind that Albertanus never produced the kind of *summa* that might have systematized his thought and made his contributions evident to his contemporaries and posterity. The treatises and sermons that followed the *De amore* were fragmented and focused on specific problems. In the case of the sermons, they were addressed to a particular audience—members of legal confraternities. Despite these difficulties, there is a coherence to the entire corpus of Albertanus's writings that has been largely overlooked and that sheds additional light on the development of his thought.

The years following the completion of the *De amore* brought a greater professional reputation to Albertanus as well as service outside his native city. During this period, his ideas were beginning to be known at least within the milieu of north Italian judges, *causidici,* and notaries. At the same time, his involvement with a legal confraternity reinforced his concerns about civic life. We have already discussed the popularity as well as the significance of these confraternities. In Albertanus's writings, we can grasp more concretely the way in which they promoted social and professional cohesiveness and helped to define the role of professionals in communal society.

These concerns are evident in the sermon he delivered before a congregation of Genoese notaries and *causidici* in the home of Petrus de Nigro, a Genoese *causidicus,* on 6 December 1243.[1] The purpose of the sermon is evident from its title, "Super confirmatione vitae illorum [On the confirmation of their life]." The opening words of the sermon, "Congregatio nostra sit in nomine Domini . . . [Let our meeting be in the name of the Lord]," establish a relationship between *confirmatio vitae* and the confraternity of judges and notaries.[2] The former defines the purpose of the latter. This sermon, as well as those delivered later in Brescia, shows the intensity of Albertanus's feeling in being a member of a professional group in the early thirteenth century. Whether or not Albertanus was university educated, his writings reflect the professional commitment that also underlay university studies at this time.[3] Given the close links between this sermon and his treatise, *De doctrina dicendi et tacendi,* it is not surprising that some professional concerns found in the sermon are also present in this treatise. The *De doctrina* helps us better to understand the relationship between his involvement in a legal confraternity and his conception of the good citizen, which emerges most clearly in the *Liber consolationis et consilii.*

The theme of professional responsibility found throughout the Genoese sermon raises an important question about the role of officials in the life of the Italian communes. In the thirteenth century, many if not most

of these officials were professionals. Although the most obvious developments were in the legal profession and have received considerable scholarly
attention, this trend also included lay officials such as the podestàs, who
were called by the communes to rule their cities.⁴ Already at the beginning
of the thirteenth century, members of the urban aristocracy had begun to
carve out careers for themselves through their service as podestàs. At Brescia, for example, members of such families as the Martinengo and the de
Madiis (Maggi) played prominent roles as podestàs in other communes as
well as participating actively in the affairs of Brescia. During the thirteenth
century, there was no more prominent example than that of the Maggi,
who dominated the city during the latter part of the century in the persons
of Bishop Berardus and Federico di Maggi. Albertanus had close relations
with this family, demonstrated by his service in the retinue of Emmanuel
de Madiis, podestà of Genoa in 1243, which provided the occasion for the
Genoese sermon.⁵

Albertanus begins by addressing his fellow *causidici* and notaries in
the words of Saint Matthew's Gospel: "You are the salt of the earth, and
if the salt shall vanish how will it be salted. For nothing more can be done
save to throw it away and let men trample on it."⁶ How does this quotation fit the professional roles of the *causidici* and notaries to whom it is
addressed? They are salt because "just as Christians are led by the Apostles
back to the flavor of faith and the sweetness of eternal life, so also through
you and your wisdom all the acts of men are brought to you for your
counsel or help, for the flavor of reason and the salt of justice, as well as
for the sweetness of the precepts of the law." And, in a way that is characteristic of his thinking, he reminds them that just as priests put salt in
the mouth of the newly baptized to profit them for the eternal life, you
should have the salt of wisdom in your mouth "that you may know how
to respond to anyone."⁷ Albertanus identifies the legal profession with
wisdom, defined as the "knowledge of the perfect good of the human
mind and of divine and human affairs." But unless this knowledge is
spread, it will vanish: "Therefore knowledge should be disseminated and
discussed so that it may be added to and increased."⁸ Rhetoric represents
the professional tool of men of law, for whom the power of language
stands at the juncture of ethical commitment and professional training.

The essence of the legal profession lies in giving advice and assistance,
especially by speaking well.⁹ Albertanus stresses the importance of sweet
speech in multiplying friendships, returning to the theme of love and
friendship that was central to the *De amore*. Here, however, his emphasis

is on speech as an instrument of the man of law. His profound respect for speech as a means to effect moral change comes through not merely in the positive value he has placed upon beautiful words, but also in his use of quotations from Saint Paul and Seneca to the effect that evil conversation corrupts good morals.[10] In his view, there is a close tie between good composition and morality.[11] Likewise, he stresses the importance of knowledge to speech. He inveighs against those who speak obscurely or ambiguously or who use sophistic words, as well as those who speak with intent to deceive. There is nothing new in the content of the advice that he gives, but his professional concern is very much a recent development.[12] And despite the fact that he is addressing notaries and *causidici*, he does not build his arguments regarding professional privileges and obligations from the usual citations to Roman law that his audience would have recognized.[13]

Albertanus advises those in the practice of law to ensure that what concerns each party is both true and sincere as well as something of consequence. They must further work to contain emotional disturbances and make appetites obedient to reason. Finally, they ought to use the goods they acquire from the practice of their profession moderately and wisely.[14] His stress on truth goes to the substance of things. His special concern is with those professionals who pursue their cause with lies rather than by the strength of the actual claim made by the litigant. The honesty of the professional is of primary importance. But Albertanus is also concerned whether the case is one that can be brought to a good effect. He warns that some things seem "good in the beginning from which many evils flow."[15]

He harkens back to the *De amore* for an example of due caution in containing emotions and appetites: "For in the business proposed to us we ought to recur to God and our conscience and, in the manner of the rooster who beats itself three times with its wings when it sings," give due deliberation to the matters proposed.[16] He condemns attempts to influence the minds of judges and others by hatred, by pleas, or by fear and envy. Though his advice is conventional, warning against favoring friends and fear of the powerful, the absence of legal references in this section of the sermon is somewhat surprising. This absence is even more striking in the section that follows, which deals with the morality of compensation for legal representation, a subject on which there was both lively debate and voluminous literature in this period.

Having stressed the importance of moderation in the use of goods, a point in keeping with his previous stance in the *De amore* and generally in accord with the ideals common among religious confraternities, Albertanus continues the sermon by arguing that it is wrong to become rich at the expense of the needy. He quotes Cassiodorus (ca. A.D. 487–ca. A.D. 580): "It is beyond all belief to wish to become wealthy from the neediness of the poor." For this reason, he argues that legal professionals have an obligation to help orphans, widows, and miserable persons "gratis and not for money." The standards that Albertanus holds before his fellow professionals are high.[17] With reason and justice as their guides, legal professionals are to live honorably, to injure no one, and give to each his due. Their reward is a good reputation, which reminds us again of the importance that Albertanus attached to the pursuit of happiness in this life in the *De amore.*

Amor civium, the love of one's fellow citizens, provided an important motivation for the thirteenth-century legal class to render service to society. Far from being an impediment to good morals, a sense of honor was essential to the community. On the other hand, as Albertanus reminds his hearers, "men hate those whom they fear."[18] Nothing could be more foolish "in a free city" than to desire to be feared. Finally, in the closing section of his sermon, he addresses the *causidici* and notaries with words that remind them that he is one of them. Again, he tells them that they are the salt of the earth, who season almost all human acts and give them the flavor of firmness, and that without their profession the laity could put nothing in writing. If the salt should vanish, they will not be good judges or good defenders. Nor will they be wise men. If notaries are not ethical they will be mere tricksters and forgers. Unless judges and other men of law practice their professions honestly, they can be expected to be ejected not only from the company of men but also from that of the devils in hell.[19]

In Albertanus's sermon, urban officials and legal professionals take on an almost priestly status, subsumed in the notion that they are a special group, "the salt of the earth." Their profession has its special language and moral obligations that separate it from the rest of the laity. It performs a special office for them much as the sacred priesthood does. Thus in the Genoese sermon Albertanus develops further his analogies between the worlds of the sacred and the secular. Even *fama,* or reputation, has its sacred counterpart in the concept of holiness. As in the *De amore,* the concept of *propositum* provides a living canvas on which to depict the medieval moral heritage's capacity for social transformation; the Genoese sermon and even more the *De doctrina dicendi et tacendi* stress the transformational power of language.

The *De doctrina,* composed in 1245, only two years after the Genoese sermon, was dedicated to Albertanus's son Stephen. It was closely dependent on the Genoese sermon, as is evident from textual similarities. Moreover, its allusion to Stephen's desire "to speak" may refer to his choice of the legal profession.[20] But the *De doctrina* must also be read against the background of Book I, chapter 2 of the *De amore,* entitled "De locutione et cohibendo spiritu et lingua cohercenda [On speech, restraining the spirit, and controlling the tongue]."[21] The relationship between the *De doctrina* and this chapter of the *De amore* is evident from Albertanus's use of a quotation from the Epistle of Saint James (3:7–8) in both, as well as in the similar content with this section of the *De amore.*[22] Thus his general idea for the *De doctrina* evolved in the course of his studies leading up to the *De amore.*

In our discussion of Albertanus's sermon to the Genoese *causidici* and notaries, we have stressed his failure to make use of legal sources that bore on his topic. A similar pattern, with some exceptions, emerges in the *De doctrina.* Even more surprising in light of the subject matter, he makes sparing use of the *ars dictaminis* and *artes praedicandi,* and, to the limited degree that he shows familiarity, he seems to have drawn on earlier works rather than on the writings of near contemporaries. Given his use of recent moral treatises, it seems significant that he did not make use of the rhetorical writings of the *De amicitia* of his contemporary, Boncompagno da Signa, or other Bolognese masters of the *ars dictaminis.*[23] As we have seen, Aldo Checchini has tried to prove that Albertanus was acquainted with the works of the Bolognese *dictatores,* but he succeeds at best in showing that Albertanus had some knowledge of the contemporary *ars,* though from what source remains uncertain.[24] What is clear is that Albertanus's writings reflected influences and sources that found little place among contemporary legal scholars and students of rhetoric. He appears certainly much more independent of such influences than if he had been a product of Bologna or Padua. Perhaps it is his educational limitations that circumscribe his use of sources and reinforce the linkages that are so evident in all his writings.

One of the prominent sources for sections 5 and 6 of the *De doctrina* is Alcuin's (A.D. 735–804) *Dialogue de arte rhetorica.*[25] Alcuin is not cited in the *De amore.*[26] On the other hand, the *De amore* does contain a few quotations from Cicero's *De inventione* though these may have come from other sources.[27] In the *De doctrina,* Albertanus does use many of the sources he did in the *De amore* and his sermon to the Genoese notaries, with the notable exceptions of the *Moralium dogma philosophorum* and to some degree the letters of Seneca. His citations from other classical and medieval sources include a strong preference for Cicero among the Classics, and for Martin of Braga, Cassiodorus, and Petrus Alfonsi among the Christian writers, all of whom he had used earlier.[28] He continues to make extensive use of the Wisdom literature from the Old Testament. As we have noted, citations from legal sources occur infrequently. This evidence seems further to confirm that Albertanus was more deeply than widely read and argues against the idea that he studied for any lengthy period in a university. But it does not rule out the possibility that he spent some time at a center other than Brescia, suggested by his use of sources which, so far as we can now tell, do not appear to have been readily available in local libraries.

The structure of the *De doctrina* was primarily influenced by rhetorical tradition. Albertanus tells us that he proposes to comment and explain each of those terms—"Quis, quid, cui dicas, cur, quomodo, quando"— that form the basis for understanding human speech and the rules governing it.[29] Like most of his contemporaries, Albertanus was in love with words and delighted in word-play. Thus he tells his readers

> Dico tibi, ut non solum quaeras a te ipso, sed requiras, id est iterum quaeras; nam istud reiterationem denotat, ut dicas *requiras,* id est iterum quaeras. Sicut enim repetere dicitur quis, hoc est iterum petere, ita requirere dicitur quis, id est iterum quaerere.

> [I tell you that you should not only ask, but require, that is ask again; for that denotes a repetition, so that you say you require, that is, ask again. For just as someone is said to repeat, that is, to petition again, so someone is said to require, that is, to ask again.][30]

Behind this linguistic word-play lies a serious effort to understand the nature and role of language in human society.

The *De doctrina* is an enquiry into the nature of social relationships through an analysis of the uses of language. Much is traditional. As we have noted, Albertanus drew on acceptable authorities. Nor was his approach to an understanding of society through the medium of language unusual. Wisdom literature and classical moral treatises abound in advice about curbing the tongue, restraining one's words, or using language to attain a desired social end. Albertanus seems to have gone further, however, in trying to apply these rules in a more systematic way to the needs of a professional group involved in the legal system of communal Italy. Without inventing anything that we can call new, Albertanus classifies the use of language into moral categories. A fascinating example of the manner in which he does this emerges directly from the first section of his treatise, entitled "Quis es qui loqueris [Who you are who would speak]."[31] The matter is indeed profound. It asks nothing less than the identity of the speaker in relation to the subject under discussion. Is the speaker directly concerned in this matter? Albertanus is addressing an increasingly popular legal concept ultimately based on Roman law: "Quod omnes tangit ab omnibus approbetur." He does not refer to it in precise terms, but there can be no doubt that it informs his discussion. But as is often the case in his approach, he takes a radically different tack and argues that one ought not to "involve oneself in a subject that is not one's business."

> As the rule of law says: thus there is blame for saying what is not one's business. Wherefore Solomon said in the Book of Proverbs: He is like one who grabbed a dog by his ears as he was passing and involved himself in the argument of another! And Jesus, son of Sirach said: "Don't get involved in an affair that doesn't concern you." Wherefore a certain one:
> What doesn't concern you in no way should cause you concern.

Or, to provide the Latin text in order to clarify the point:

> ut dicit regula iuris: ita culpa est loqui istud, *quod ad se non pertineat.* Unde Salomo in Proverbiis dixit: Sicut qui apprehendit auribus canem, ita qui transit et impatiens commiscetur alterius rixae. Et Jesus filius Sidrach dixit: De ea re, que te non molestat, ne certaveris. Unde quidam:
> *Quod te non tangit,* hoc te nullatenus angit.[32] (Italics mine.)

"Quod omnes tangit" had a special significance in the communal life of northern Italy in the late twelfth and early thirteenth centuries. It provided a legal foundation for the representative and proctorial institutions that were emerging not only within the cities but also from the relationships between the cities and other centers of power, for example, the sovereign king-emperors. While it is possible to read Albertanus merely as advising his son to mind his own business, the language suggests knowledge of the legal maxim, using *Quod omnes tangit* to warn against unwarranted interference in the affairs of others as a cause of factionalism and internal violence in the cities.

The *De doctrina* echoes Albertanus's first sermon in its concern about the role of the legal profession. Its dedication to Stephen suggests, as we have noted above, that it was intended as a manual for a young man preparing for a profession in the law and public affairs, but it also fits in with the public and urban character that we have identified in the *De amore*. Perhaps this aspect had a special meaning to contemporaries, as the following passage, probably an interpolation, suggests:

> Therefore, before you blame another, you should take care to be innocent of similar vices; and [Pope] Gregory confirmed this saying: Let him who is anguished over sins be a foreigner to sin, after the example of Christ, who absolved the woman taken in adultery and freed her from the very evil Jews, who accused her and judged her to be a sinner, although they were guilty of serious crimes. Here judges, both secular and spiritual, should be terrified to be fornicators, adulterers, greedy, unjust, of whom Solomon said: "The hardest judgment will be for those in charge; and it follows that the powerful will suffer torments more powerfully."[33]

The *De doctrina's* character as a professional manual was, therefore, apparent in its own time. In the stages of development from the *De amore* and the Genoese sermon, it also seems possible that the relationship between religious rule and social change was present in the analogy between *congregatio* and *civitas* in the Genoese sermon and the *De doctrina*.

As in his sermon to the Genoese notaries, Albertanus in the *De doctrina* places special emphasis on truth as the object of enquiry. It is the "quid" that guides speech. "Above all things, truth, which makes men neighbors to God, must be cultivated."[34] Marshalling his authorities in support of truth, Albertanus returns to the issue of oath-taking, previously addressed in the *De amore*. He maintains that "you ought to speak the truth so that your word will have the weight of an oath and [that] there may be no difference between your simple assertion and an oath."[35] This view differs from his earlier labelling of those refusing to take oaths as heretics. It suggests that he may well have softened his stand or at least become more sympathetic to those who refused to take oaths, asserting that their simple word should be sufficient. This line of thought is strengthened by his statement that "even if God is not invoked in an oath and not summoned to witness, still you should not transgress the truth nor neglect the law of justice." But Albertanus recognizes the necessity for some lies that serve as guardians of truth. Such lies are excused because their cause is honest. They are in the interest of the community. "The just man does not give up secrets. For he keeps silence about matters requiring silence and speaks about those where he needs to speak and so there is a fit peace and a secure tranquillity for him."[36] Speaking the truth must stand the test of reason. "He who carries reason with him conquers the whole world," Albertanus says, paraphrasing Seneca in a quotation he had previously used in his Genoese sermon. Indeed, this sermon seems never to have been far from his thoughts as he wrote the *De doctrina*.[37]

The communal focus of Albertanus's thought is developed in the seventh and eighth points of the second section of the *De doctrina*. Point Seven deals with words or actions that cause injury. His concerns about violence provoke him to say that "injuries and contumelies are so very evil, that not only do they injure individuals but also cities and kingdoms, which suffer because of disturbances and revolutions [mutationes]."[38] Yet he recognizes that it is not always possible to withdraw from violence. Though he counsels those engaged in disturbances to cease, he says that they should do so only if they can avoid substantial loss.[39] His approach to internal disorder acknowledges that some losses cannot be permitted.

In Point Eight, Albertanus advises that "nothing is more pernicious in a city than sedition; where there is sedition, there is factionalism."[40] This statement goes beyond a condemnation of communal violence such as might be expected from one of Albertanus's background and experience. It reflects the structure and purpose of the *De doctrina* as a treatise about the empowering of a professional class to examine critically the role of language in the preservation or destruction of order within the commune. But this message is not found with discussions of offices and responsibilities, as was the case, for example, in the podestà literature written about this same time. Albertanus has preserved an angle of vision that is not directed from concern about institutions and law, but instead concern about the responsibilities of individual members of a profession to the community.

In the view of Albertanus, language was a tool that expressed relationships within the community. It possessed an ethical meaning that flowed directly from its power to affect society and individuals. The study of rhetoric involved fundamental ethical issues that touched on the nature of civil society. If we seek affinities between medieval and Renaissance approaches to language, one key would certainly be in the concept of language as power.[41] For Albertanus the connection between language and power was basic to his view of the legal profession in the *De doctrina*. Language had its skilled practitioners, on whom it conferred power in human affairs. This political dimension of language was never far from

Albertanus's thought. He was aware not only of its force for the public good, but also of its capacity to destroy the weak and the poor, or even the rich and powerful. His recognition of the power of language and his effort to provide a guide to its moral use was fundamental not merely to the advice he gave, but also to the formal structure of his treatise, which depended on his use of rhetoric to put analysis of language into a philosophical framework.

The power of language forms a major theme of Albertanus's work. In the fourth section of his treatise, dealing with *Cur loquendum sit*—that is, with the final cause or reasons for speech—Albertanus presents two main reasons, defined as the service of God and human convenience. Under service of God, he lists secular and spiritual preachers. The terminology may refer to preaching by laity and the clergy.[42] If so, his own preaching would fall into the former category. Under human convenience, he places "*causidici* and other orators."[43] Thus his professional advice served as an example of social service while his preaching represented his "service of God."

From the concept of service, it is but a short step to the idea of reward. The final definition of a profession is actually based on its way of rewarding its practitioners. The issue was posed in the patristic age in terms of the tangible value of language, which was the medium by which professionals provided their service. It was a problem that had special meaning for teachers and lawyers. The idea that words had value must be seen in terms analogous to the relationship between language and power. This idea lay at the root of Albertanus's discussion of the legitimacy of professional payments to lawyers and legal experts.[44] Citing Augustine, the usual authority in favor of such payments, Albertanus defended the acceptance of moderate fees while, as he had done in his sermon to the Genoese notaries, he condemned the taking of fees from those in need, citing Cassiodorus to support this view.

In the hands of professionals, every aspect of language is relevant to the use of power for good or for evil. Pronunciation and clarity of delivery affect the manner in which speech persuades an audience. Speed and slowness in speech reflect the quality of mind of the speaker. Judges "should be slow" in judging. "This is a royal virtue . . . For it is written: I think that he judges best who understands quickly and judges slowly."[45] Judges should be men of few words, but when they speak, their words should be joyful, honest, lucid, simple, delivered with face composed and without loud laughter and without any clamor. The relationship between the form and content of speech expresses that between language and morality.

"Quando Loquendum et Dicendum Sit, et Quo Ordine [When and in what order one must speak]" sets forth rules to govern speech and silence. Silence is as important as speech. Keeping silent is the exercise of moral control over the power of language to do good or evil. Albertanus quotes Petrus Alfonsi: "Do not hasten to answer until there is an end of the questioning."[46] He illustrates the notion of a proper time and place for speaking by discussing the various forms of speech and the main requirements for each. He begins with preaching, and details briefly the need for history, allegory, and tropology in the construction of a sermon. He speaks of letters, listing the various parts of the letter as they are found in the standard treatises of dictamen but without providing an indication of a particular source. He speaks of diplomacy, a subject to which he devotes rather more space than to preaching or letter writing. Its importance in the Italian cities of the thirteenth century and its relationship to his own profession and his own experience may well explain this emphasis. He gives precise instructions for a spokesman accompanying an embassy. After devoting three points to the salutation and commendation of those to whom the embassy is directed, he proceeds:

> you will make an exhortation by speaking persuasive words to obtain that which is sought. Fourth, by alleging moderation in every demand by which that which is sought can be accomplished. Fifth, you will bring out examples of things done and observed in similar negotiations, and finally, in sixth place, you will assign a sufficient reason for all the aforesaid matters. And you will do this according to the example of the Archangel Gabriel, who when he was sent by God to the Blessed Virgin Mary, first greeted her, saying: "Hail, full of grace, the Lord be with you: Blessed are you," etc. Secondly, he gave comfort or exhortation from God: Do not be afraid Mary: and the archangel put this exhortation before the announcement, because Mary had been disturbed by the salutation of the archangel. Third, he put the announcement, saying: Behold you will conceive in your womb, and you will bring forth a son, etc. Fourth, he described how when he said: The Holy Spirit will come over you, and the power of the Most High will overshadow you. Fifth, he set forth an example, when he said: Behold Elizabeth, your cousin, will bear a son in her old age. Sixth, he assigned a sufficient cause when he said that no word is impossible with God.[47]

The use of the angelic salutation as an example illustrates Albertanus's tendency to draw on his religious experience to explain a secular activity. The negotiation carried on by the professional representative of a ruler was put into a sacred context, much as he had characterized the legal profession in the Genoese sermon in quasi-priestly terms as "the salt of the earth." The special vocation of professionals was emphasized in the *De doctrina* as in his earlier writings.

"The life of literate men consists rather in speech and in speaking than in doing."[48] This parting advice of Albertanus to his son provides a basic insight into his view of the nature of society. It was to urban professionals that he had addressed his sermon to the Genoese notaries and his treatise *De doctrina dicendi et tacendi*. There can be little doubt that it was from the experience of urban life and from the moral imperatives of urban discourse that his concern for language received its impetus. Albertanus subordinated his concerns about linguistic form to ethical goals. That this connection did not go unrecognized in the work of later thinkers may be understood by the fact that Brunetto Latini arranged the materials he borrowed from the *De doctrina* under his own treatment of the virtue of prudence.[49] The ethical significance of language was well understood by one of the major encyclopedists of the thirteenth century.

The relationship of this treatise to a rising sense of professionalism in thirteenth-century Europe and to the urban environment of northern Italy has been little noticed. Earlier scholars have tried to place Albertanus within the framework of the major intellectual movements of the period, whether the Senecan tradition or that of the pre-humanists. While some relationship to these movements is evident, and, in fact, accounts for the tendency of scholars to attempt to make these linkages, Albertanus does not really fit into any of these categories. He appears isolated from many of the main trends of his time, while at the same time at least peripherally aware of them. He had no predecessors and few direct successors. In order to understand him we must expand the parameters of our enquiry. We must explore his position not merely in relation to the intellectual movements of the age but in his relation to the commune as a social unit.

Albertanus's commitment to the commune was based upon its nature and the problems inherent in its structures. Applying his understanding of the power of language, he attempted to explain why factionalism was so rife in the cities. But he did not stop merely with a recognition of the problems and their relationship to his own profession. He also recognized that the moral aspect of language had a special meaning to the city and to the solution of its problems. Hence, he stressed the moral element in treating the relationship between language and his profession. In his sermon of 1243 and in the *De doctrina* of 1245, Albertanus focused chiefly on one aspect of the study that he had begun in the *De amore*. If the *De amore* was a plan of life, then the *De doctrina* was a career guide for the public man, especially the public man in the service of the Italian commune. As such, it was an authentic voice of an emerging professionalism both in terms of its ideals and its problems.

The *De doctrina*, taken in conjunction with other writings of Albertanus, is among the earliest and most extensive bodies of writing by a layman on the subject of professionalism. Unlike discussions in legal sources, the work of Albertanus is concerned with the social meaning of professional life, namely the relation of the professional man to the community. His sense of participation in all aspects of community life extends well beyond most of the political writings of the period, which tend to focus on offices, public obligations, and the public character of official life. Albertanus pays little attention to this aspect of professional life, though his occasional references reveal his awareness of it. This is especially evident in his discussion of diplomatic negotiations. But that account also shows that his real concern was with the manner in which public life was carried out. He confers a special dignity on those engaged in this activity.

During this period, Albertanus's concerns about his profession, expressed to both his colleagues and his sons, dominate his thinking and writings. His profession serves as a bond uniting his participation in the confraternity of notaries and *causidici* and his participation in the life of the *civitas*. He obviously looks to the professionals of his class and group to bring about a community based on good moral principles. Whereas in the *De amore* he stressed the concept of voluntary acceptance of a rule as a guide to a *beata vita*, he now stresses the role of professional judges and advocates in achieving this end. He tries to define professionalism in moral terms. It is the particular role of the professional to work with all of the various segments of the community in order to promote good order and peaceful resolution of disputes. Lawyers, *causidici*, and judges are practitioners of language. Language here has a meaning that goes beyond the limits of ordinary discourse. It is speech rooted in the tradition of public discourse; speech that affects the community. This is the meaning of professional speech.

At the same time, he is aware of other effects of speech within the community. He speaks, for example, of the destructive power of language that produces factionalism. When he wrote the *Liber consolationis et consilii* in 1246, he focused on the vendetta as a distinctive example of communal dissention. In what must be regarded as his masterwork, later adapted by Chaucer from a French version for his "Tale of Melibee," Albertanus returns once again to the *De amore* to develop a strand of thought that had been especially prominent there. But now he applies it more directly to the urban scene. If the *De amore* had broadly conceived of the basis for societal reform in a secularization of the concepts of religious rule and conversion, the *Liber Consolationis et consilii* sought to move toward a new vision of the nature of social change.

Notes

1. For recent work on confraternities in northern Italy, see Lester Little, *Liberty, Charity, Fraternity: Lay Religious Confraternities in Bergamo in the Age of the Commune* (Bergamo, 1988), 17–97. For Brescia, there is as yet no complete account, but see Antonino Mariella, *Le origini degli ospedali bresciani* (Brescia, 1963), 22–25 and 139–40; *Le pergamene degli Umiliati di Cremona*, ed. Vincenzo d'Alessandro (Palermo, 1964), 73; John R. H. Moorman, *A History of the Franciscan Order from its Origins to the Year 1517* (Oxford, 1968) 218–19; Paolo Guerrini, "Gli statuti di un'antica congregazione Francescana di Brescia," *Archivum Franciscanum Historicum* 1 (1908): 544–47; *Ordo fraternitatis* 1:410–34, 3:1373–89.

2. *Sermone inedito di Albertano, guidice di Brescia*, ed. Luigi F. Fè d'Ostiani (Brescia, 1874), 33.

3. On his attitude toward his profession, see ibid., 46–47, and *Sermones quattuor*, 10, 41–43, 61, 63.

4. *Oculus Pastoralis* 4:95–148, esp. 99–102. See also Quentin Skinner, "Political Philosophy," in *The Cambridge History of Renaissance Philosophy*, ed. Charles Schmitt, 389–91 (Cambridge, 1988). His argument that "the city-state remained an anomaly within the legal structures of thirteenth-century Europe" appears to me to be misleading, because one could easily infer from it that the development of the city-state had no influence on other polities or on the development of western political theory.

5. Marta Ferrari, "Intorno ad alcuni sermoni inediti di Albertano da Brescia," *Atti del istituto veneto di scienze, lettere ed arti* 109 (1950–51): 72. On Emmanuel de Madiis (Maggi), see *LP* 19:476, 503, 644, and *Annales Parmenses maiores*, *MGHSS* 18:676, which states that he was podestà of Parma in 1251. For his service as a Roman Senator in 1256 and 1257, see *Codice diplomatico del senato romano dal MCXLIV al MCCCXLVII*, 214–24. See also Ferdinand Gregorovius, *History of the City of Rome in the Middle Ages*, 6 vols. (London, 1908–12), 5:1, 318–21.

6. *Sermone inedito*, 34. Aside from the references to these works in manuscripts as sermons, their form is evident. However, only two of the sermons—this one and the third sermon in his Brescian collection—open with Biblical quotations. *Sermones quattuor*, 37.

7. Ibid., 35.

8. Ibid.

9. On the medieval art of rhetoric, consult James J. Murphy, *Rhetoric in the Middle Ages: A History of Rhetorical Theory from Saint Augustine to the Renaissance* (Berkeley, Cal., 1974) and his *Medieval Rhetoric: A Select Bibliography* (Toronto, 1989). Murphy notes that the fourteenth-century *Les Leys d'Amors* of Guilhelm Molinier and his associates in the *Consistoire du Gai Savoir* drew on "Brunetto Latini, Albertano da Brescia, Alexander of Villedieu, Priscian, and Donatus." (Murphy, *Rhetoric*, 115)

10. *Sermone inedito*, 37.

11. Cicero, Marcus Tullius, *De inventione* (Cambridge, Mass., 1968) 1:1, sustains the position taken by Albertanus.

12. James A. Brundage, "The Medieval Advocate's Profession," *Law and History Review* 6 (1988): 439–64.

13. *Sermone inedito*, 38.

14. Ibid., 38–39.

15. Ibid., 40.

16. Ibid., 40.

17. Ibid., 43.

18. Ibid., 45–46.

19. Ibid., 45–47; Sundby, *Liber*, 120–21.

20. Sundby, *De doctrina*, 479.

21. Sharon Hiltz, "*De amore et dilectione Dei et proximi et aliarum rerum et de forma vitae*. An Edition" (Ph.D. diss., University of Pennsylvania, 1980), 7–18.

22. Ibid., 7–8.

23. Ludwig Rockinger, ed., *Briefsteller und Formelbücher des elften bis vierzehnten Jahrhunderts*, Quellen und Erörterungen zur bayerischen und deutschen Geschichte, vol. 9 (Munich, 1863), 125–26. Boncampagno da Signa's statute for a religious rule for a lay confraternity would surely have attracted the attention of Albertanus. But here, as in the case of Boncompagno's *Amicitia*, there is no evidence of direct influence on Albertanus. Gérard G. Meersseman, "Per la storiografia delle confraternite nel medioevo," *Ordo Fraternitatis* 1:3–34, esp. 18–21. For further discussion of Boncompagno, see Robert L. Benson, "Protohumanism and Narrative Technique in Early Thirteenth-Century 'Ars Dictaminis,'" *Boccaccio: Secoli di vita, Atti del congresso internazionale: Boccaccio, 1975*, ed. Marga Cottino-Jones and Edward Tuttle (Ravenna, 1977), 31–48.

24. Aldo Checchini, "Un giudice del secolo decimertzo: Albertano da Brescia," *Atti del reale istituto veneto di scienze, lettere ed arti* 71:2 (1911–12): 24; Ferrari, "Intorno," 81–82.

25. Sundby, *De doctrina*, 498–506; Alcuin, *De Rhetorica: The Rhetoric of Alcuin and Charlemagne* (Princeton, 1941), 138–40.

26. Hiltz, "*De amore*," 326.

27. Ibid., 328.

28. Ibid., 326–41. This list of citations certainly represents a fair sample of the works used by Albertanus in the *De amore* as well as in his other writings.

29. Sundby, *De doctrina*, 479; Cicero, *De inventione* 1:24–26; *Rhetores latini minores*, ed. Carolus Halm (Leipzig, 1863), 103, 141; Alcuin, *De rhetorica*, 70; and

Thierry of Chartres, *The Latin Rhetorical Commentaries,* ed. Karen M. Fredborg (Toronto, 1988), 52, 139. Santino Caramella, "Dante e Albertano da Brescia," *Studi letterari: Miscellanea in onore di Emilio Santini* (Palermo, 1956), 87–94, esp. 88–89, has located the source of "cui dicas" in Gilbert de la Porrée's *Liber de sex principiis* (Münster, 1953).

30. Sundby, *De doctrina,* 479.

31. Ibid., 480.

32. Ibid. Italics mine. For a discussion of "Quod omnes tangit," see Gaines Post, "A Romano-Canonical Maxim, *Quod omnes tangit,* in Bracton and Early Parliaments," *Studies in Medieval Legal Thought* (Princeton, 1964), 163–238, esp. 170–72; Brian Tierney, *Religion, Law and the Growth of the Constitutional Thought, 1150–1650* (Cambridge, 1983), 21–28. But see Milan, Biblioteca Ambrosiana, B. 40 Sup., which omits the second quotation. Perhaps it was added to strengthen the reference to "quod omnes tangit."

33. "Priusquam igitur alium culpes, a vitiis similibus innocens esse cures; quod idem Gregorius confirmavit dicens: Qui alium arguit de peccatis, a peccatis debet esse alienus, exemplo Christi, qui mulierem in adulterio deprehensam absolvit et liberavit a pessimis Judaeis, qui accusabant et judicabant peccatricem, quum ipsimet scelerosissimi forent. Terreantur hic judices fornicarii, adulteri, avari, injusti, tam spirituales, quam saeculares, de quibus ait Salomo: Judicium durissimum fiet his qui praesunt; et sequitur: quoniam potentes potenter tormenta patientur." Sundby, *De doctrina,* 483. Vatican City, BAV, Vat. Lat. 991 has omitted this entire passage. Milan, Biblioteca Ambrosiana, B. 40 Sup. also omits this passage.

34. Ibid., 485. "Super omnia enim veritas est colenda, quae sola Deo homines proximos facit, quum ipse Deus veritas sit."

35. Ibid. "Ita ergo veritatem loqui debes, ut dictum tuum habeat pondus jurisjurandi, et nihil intersit inter tuum simplicem assertionem et jusjurandum."

36. Ibid. " . . . justus autem secreta non prodit, tacenda enim tacet, loquenda loquitur; atque ita apta illi pax est et secura tranquillitas."

37. Ibid., 487; Seneca, *Epistulae,* 37, 4.

38. Sundby, *De doctrina,* 488–89. "Injuriae namque et contumeliae tam pessimae sunt, ut non solum cuilibet noceant, sed et etiam civitatibus et regnis, quae propterea disturbationes et mutationes patiuntur." Of course, this observation applies to various political structures, not cities alone.

39. Ibid., 488–89.

40. Ibid., 490. " . . . nihil enim perniciosus in civitate, quam seditio; ubi seditio, ibi civium divisio."

41. Jerrold Seigel, *Rhetoric and Philosophy in Renaissance Humanism: The Union of Eloquence and Wisdom, Petrarch to Valla* (Princeton, 1968). Also Jill Meredith, "The Revival of the Augustan Age in the Court Art of Frederick II," *Artistic Strategy and the Rhetoric of Power,* ed. David Castriota (Carbondale, Ill., 1986), 39–56, provides a number of suggestive points in comparison to Albertanus's writings.

42. Sundby, *De Doctrina,* 496. "ut faciunt praedicatores saeculares et spirituales."

43. Ibid.

44. *Sermone inedito,* 40–41.

45. Sundby, *De doctrina,* 501.

46. Ibid., 503.

47. Ibid., 504–5. " . . . facies exhortationem dicendo suasoria verba ad consequendum id, quod postulatur, quarto in omni postulatione allegando modum, quo id, quod postulatur, fieri valeat. Quinto induces exempla de rebus in similibus negotiis factis et observatis. Sexto denique assignabis sufficientem rationem ad praedicta omnia. Et hoc facias ad exemplum Gabrielis archangeli, qui, quum missus esset a Deo ad beatam virginem Mariam, primo posuit salutationem dicens: Ave gratia plena: Dominus tecum: Benedicta tu etc. Secundo confortationem sive exhortationem de Deo: Ne timeas Maria: Quam exhortationem praeposuit archangelus denuntiationi, et hoc ideo, quia beata Maria turbata fuerat in salutatione archangeli. Tertio vero posuit annuntiationem dicens: Ecce concipies in utero, et paries filium etc. Quarto posuit modi expressionem, quum dixit: Spiritus sanctus superveniet in te, et virtus Altissimi obumbrabit tibi. Quinto posuit exemplum, quum dixit: Ecce Elizabeth, cognata tua, pariet filium in senectute sua. Sexto assignavit sufficientem rationem ad praedicta, quum dixit: Quia non erit impossibile apud Deum omne verbum." Vatican City, BAV, Vat. Lat. 991 has dicendo for Deo: "Missus esset a Deo."

48. Ibid. 505.

49. Brunetto Latini, *Li livres dou tresor,* ed. Francis J. Carmody (Berkeley, Cal., 1948), 236–45.

4. The Attack on the Vendetta

ALBERTANUS'S RETURN from Genoa and his authorship of the *De doctrina dicendi et tacendi* mark a midpoint in his writing career. But little is known of his public career during this phase of his life. On 13 August 1249, he witnessed an agreement that he may have taken part in as a notary in 1236.[1] The only other documents that provide evidence of his professional involvement and status in this period are concerned with a treaty between Brescia and Bergamo on 4 May and 11 May 1251.[2] Although it seems probable that he spent the years between 1243 and 1249 in Brescia, he may also have continued to serve Emmanuel de Madiis (Maggi) or other Brescians during their periods as podestàs in other north Italian cities. This was also a period of intense conflict between the emperor and the communes in northern Italy, but there is no direct tie between Albertanus and the military campaigns against Frederick II or any evidence of his involvement with the diplomacy of the period other than that already noted. Given his earlier activities, the lack of documentation for these years might suggest that he was less active in public life. A partial explanation may be found in his writings and in his participation in the confraternity of *causidici* in Brescia. In his writings, he continued to pursue the plan he had outlined in the *De amore*. As we have already seen, his Genoese sermon and the *De doctrina dicendi et tacendi* both had close ties with the *De amore*. This relationship is also evident in the *Liber consolationis et consilii,* which he completed in 1246. Dedicated to his son John, a surgeon, this treatise extended the analysis of conflict and vendetta that Albertanus had begun in the *De amore*.[3]

The *De amore* had offered a broad vision for the reform of society in the voluntary acceptance of a certain body of rules, a way of life. The achievement of this state was placed in the hands of a body of professionals devoted to the practice of wisdom, as is evident in the *De doctrina,* which provides an extensive commentary on the professional role of those who would advise their fellow citizens and expands in practical ways on the critical issue of how reform is to occur. Embryonic in this treatise is a notion of those professionals as a secular priesthood, an idea that would undergo further development in later medieval thought as a result of legal studies in the *Digest* of Justinian.[4]

In the *Liber consolationis et consilii*, Albertanus examines the causes of violence and advances means for its resolution, which in his opinion are to be found in the secularization of an essential priestly power. The relationship between the legal profession and the priesthood is more sharply drawn in the *Liber consolationis et consilii* than in his earlier writings. While I speak of this process in terms of secularization, however, it is important to inject a word of caution. I am not here suggesting the hoary bifurcation of secular and sacred that bedevils modern thought. Such a notion was totally absent in Albertanus. He had a rather different view, one shared with his contemporaries, in which secular referred merely to one sphere of human activity while spiritual concerned another. To the degree that these were separate, it was possible to conceive of secular as emerging from the ordinary concerns of the laity organized in civil society. Despite the fact that there was clear tension in medieval society between temporal and spiritual authority—between church and state—Albertanus viewed secular and spiritual in complementary terms. He affirmed a tradition that was essentially dualistic but perceived no conflict between secular and spiritual goals. Thus in Albertanus's thought the possible analogies between secular and sacred were different from those generally understood in the twentieth century, but were not far removed from those that helped to shape modern thought in significant ways.[5]

The problem of violence was endemic in communal society in the thirteenth century. Writing a bit later than Albertanus, Rolandinus of Padua commenced his chronicle of his native city by descrying the cruelty of tyrants, who "destroy towers and palaces, devour riches, make orphans and widows, and destroy all property and persons."[6] This complaint, which echoed the experience of Mattheus of Corregia in the early 1220s, sounded throughout the region, especially during the period of intensive military campaigning undertaken by the forces of Ezzelino da Romano, Frederick II, and their allies. But, where Rolandinus and most of his contemporaries chose to focus on the impact of the wars of Frederick II—the example of Salimbene comes immediately to mind—Albertanus takes a different approach. Instead of writing a chronicle about violence, he seeks to understand the nature of violence through a study of the relationship of the individual to the community and a search for the causes of conflict among individuals and families. In this effort, he shows his continued ties

to twelfth-century moral literature. While continuing this tradition, however, *Liber consolationis* deals more explicitly with the urban environment
than Albertanus's other writings. But what is most important to Albertanus is the theoretical structure of his work rather than specific historical
events or contexts. He is more attuned to social theory than to politics or
history. At the same time, however, he seems very aware of the reality of
violence and its social causes. Beneath his moralizing, there is a solid foundation of experience that informs his approach. What separates him from
the twelfth-century writers of moral treatises in the Senecan tradition is
not merely his overarching structure, but also his sense of concrete experience as the basis for his moral judgments.

The *Liber consolationis* is not merely a rehash of his earlier writings;
rather it is an extension of his ideas about the causes and solutions for
violence in society, building on both the *De amore* and the *De doctrina* as
well as his related sermon to the Genoese notaries and *causidici*. There are,
for example, important differences in his use of sources, not merely in the
number of citations from particular works but also in the manner in which
they are used. Whereas Cicero and Seneca had previously accounted for
over half of the quotations from classical authors, they represent only
twenty-five percent in the *Liber consolationis*. The *Sententiae* of Publilius
Syrus, the first century B.C. author of Latin mimes, has become his most
important classical source. Also popular is the *De nugis philosophorum*,
falsely attributed to Caecilius Balbus, but which also harkens back to Publilius Syrus, and the elder Cato's *De moribus*, a collection of his thoughts
most likely compiled after his death. While Cicero's *De officiis* continues to
be cited frequently—about twenty-seven times—his *De amicitia*, which
was often cited in the *De amore*, is seldom mentioned in the *Liber consolationis*. There is no notable change in Albertanus's preferences in Old Testament sources: he cites Ecclesiasticus and Proverbs most often; more than
seventy percent of all Old Testament quotations are from these books. In
the New Testament, there are also no notable differences. Among early
medieval and patristic sources, his favorite is Martin of Braga's *Formula
honestae vitae* and *De moribus*, and, after this, Cassiodorus's *Variae*, which
together account for almost three-fourths of all the sources cited by Albertanus from this period. Among post-1100 sources, he continues to cite
Petrus Alfonsi with some frequency, but makes few references to the
Moralium dogma philosophorum. On the other hand, he cites legal sources
from both Roman and Canon law with greater frequency in *Liber consolationis* than in any of his previous writings. He also makes greater use of

the *Didascalicon* of the great twelfth-century Parisian, Hugh of St. Victor, than previously. Interesting though this summary may be, it only hints at the major differences in his use of sources in *Liber consolationis*. The *Liber consolationis* is much more concerned with law than previous treatises. This is understandable in light of its subject matter. Not only is it concerned with violence but specifically with the vendetta, that deeply entrenched custom of pursuing personal vengeance for injuries; moreover, it examines ways in which such conflicts can be resolved. Discussion of law is therefore important to the theme of the book. It is also notable that the total number of citations in the *Liber consolationis* is fewer than in his earlier works, thus providing a somewhat greater scope for the author's own ideas.[7]

The *Liber consolationis* is the only one of Albertanus's writings to take the form of a dialogue. Popular since antiquity, this form was used by medieval authors of moral treatises as well as of *artes dictaminis*, although none are cited by Albertanus. What characterizes his dialogue is that it is carried on between a husband, Melibeus, and his wife *Prudentia* or Prudence. Since Prudence assumes the leading role in advising Melibeus, it is apparent that Albertanus attached unusual importance to female advice. This alone distinguishes his treatise from others of the period. It is not merely that Albertanus placed a positive value on women, but he reversed the traditional order of relationships between men and women and did so consciously in order to emphasize certain "female" characteristics in the social order.[8] This does not mean that he was uncritical of women. Indeed, he also noted the customary female vices and warns against them in the *De amore*.[9] But the *Liber consolationis* passes over such criticisms, indeed refutes them. It may be indebted to the late Roman and Christian author, Boethius, and his use of philosophy in female guise in his *Consolatio philosophiae* [*Consolation of Philosophy*]. Indeed, the Boethian model seems to suggest the form of the *Liber consolationis*. Just as Philosophy, as a female, "the teacher of all the virtues [omnium magistra virtutum]" consoles Boethius, so *Prudentia*, the virtue that counsels wisdom, advises Melibeus.[10] In a broad sense, *Philosophia* provided Albertanus with a model for *Prudentia*, accounting perhaps in this way for the positive image that Albertanus accorded the wife of Melibeus.

But the *Consolation of Philosophy* does not seem to have been a direct model for the *Liber consolationis et consilii* in terms of content and was certainly not a major source for it. Sundby has identified only one direct citation from the *Consolation of Philosophy*.[11] Albertanus states that he is quoting the following from the second book of the *Consolation:* "Nihil enim est fortuna, nisi secundum opinionem vulgi [for fortune is nothing but the opinion of the crowd]." However, the closest quotation to this found in the *Consolation* is from Book 4, chapter 7, in which we find the phrase *opinionem populi* [popular opinion].[12] This rather free citation of Boethius casts serious doubt on the extent of Albertanus's knowledge of Boethius's work. He does not refer to the *Consolation of Philosophy* elsewhere in his treatises and sermons, and his modern editors have not located any other reference to the *Consolation.* Of course, the *Consolation of Philosophy* was a widely known work and it would be strange if Albertanus did not have some knowledge of it. Failure to cite it does not prove his ignorance; it only suggests that he did not have it at hand. However, he certainly was familiar enough to draw on it for the title of his work and very likely for the idea of a dialogue between Prudence and Melibeus.

Albertanus himself identified his source for the character of Melibeus in the *De amore.* He cited the *Epigrammata* of Godofredus Prior, or Godfrey of Winchester (1050?-1107), which, if not a favorite source, is one that he used on various occasions. Interestingly, he joins parts of two epigrams from Godofredus. The first relates to Melibeus:

> CLIV. Consilio juvenum non esse fidendum
> Consilio juvenum fidis, Melibaee, ruinam
>   Expectare potes, dum sine consilio es.

> [The counsel of the young is not to be trusted.
>   You trust the counsel of the young, Melibeus,
> You can expect ruin, because you are without counsel.][13]

This passage was only a portion of the whole verse. To it, Albertanus added another couplet:

> LIII. Consilium senum rejiciendum non esse
> Pannorum veterum facile contemnitur uses,
>   Non sic concilium, Postumiane, senum.

> [The counsel of the elders should not be rejected.
> The use of old clothes is easily set aside,
>   Not so the counsel of the old, O Postumianus.][14]

However, he apparently had another version at hand for the second line, for he wrote "Nec sic consilium, Postume sperne senum [Do not thus spurn the counsel of the old, O Postume!]."[15]

In any case, it is apparent that Godofredus Prior provided a much more direct inspiration for the choice of Melibeus as a character in his dialogue than the ultimate source of the name in the Eclogues of the classic poet Virgil.[16] The subject matter of Virgil's poem is an allegory about the triumph of Rome and its impact on the ordinary life of the shepherds and farmers of the countryside. It has no similarity to the ideas of Albertanus. Moreover, there is little likelihood that Albertanus was even aware of Virgil's Melibeus. Rather the lines from Godofredus "You trust in the counsel of the young, Melibeus; you can expect ruin, because you are without counsel," echo throughout the *Liber consolationis et consilii*. Moreover, Albertanus had been at pains to contrast the counsel of the old to that of the young in the *De amore* in a fashion similar to that he found in the two quotations from the *Epigrammata* that he joined. Thus in probing the nature of violence, Albertanus drew inspiration not merely from Boethius for the concept of a dialogue between a woman and a man, but also from Godofredus Prior for the notion that secure counsel was not easily to be found.

Like the *De amore,* the *Liber consolationis* represents a specific development within the tradition of moral treatises. The break with the twelfth-century moral tradition, which we have discussed in connection with the *De amore,* is also visible in the *Liber consolationis*. In this latter case, such a change is all the more evident because of the shift in the type of sources used. As in the case of the *De amore,* the title also signals this change by its reference to the Boethian tradition. But the strongest support comes from an internal analysis of the treatise itself. The *Liber consolationis* focuses on the urban vendetta. The evidence for its urban character is scattered but is sufficient to provide a clear context for the work. Its form as a dramatic dialogue focuses on the human relationships that lie at the root of communal violence, paying special attention to tensions arising from differences of wealth, rank, and social status. But what is chiefly new is the structure of the treatise and its effort to resolve fundamental social problems in a new way. The *Liber consolationis* tries to move beyond the societal role of the professional classes to examine that of the individual as a critical figure in the transformation of society.

The topics that dominated Albertanus's writings correspond to the pressing problems of medieval Italian urban life. His emphasis is different, however, from what we would expect from an examination of contemporary moral treatises by clerical authors.[17] There, major emphases are on issues such as usury and just price, a tendency that becomes very evident in the work of the friars during the course of the thirteenth century.[18] But Albertanus was more concerned with constructing a moral basis for ordinary life in the city. He might be characterized, with a certain justice, as a sociologist of the medieval urban experience because of his attempt to find causes and solutions to the problems of violence within the context of human relationships.

His approach springs from his conception of the city, from his sources, and from his own professional commitment. The city as a center of economic activity lay in the background of his thinking. More immediate was his sense of the implications of concentrating a population within a certain space. His focus was on the interaction of people from every stratum of society. His view was based on the physical reality of the city, in particular on the towers that dominated the Italian communal skyline in the first half of the thirteenth century. He was not naive about the role of economic differences as a cause of urban conflict. His lengthy discussions of the *potentes* and the poor, in which he linked poverty and political impotence, may be conventional but are still basic to his view of the causes of social tensions.[19] As in the *De doctrina,* however, Albertanus reserves his most extensive and penetrating analysis for his examination of the role of discourse in the resolution of social conflict.[20]

The tale of Melibeus, destined to be the most popular of Albertanus's works because of its dramatic power, is a classic statement of the plight of the individual in the fragmented society of the early thirteenth century. Melibeus is rich and powerful, perhaps self-made, certainly not one of the powerful lords who have moved from the countryside into the town, as we can conclude from the fact that he lacks the ties of kinship and lordship that marked this class. During his absence on a trip, his enemies enter his house and attack his wife and daughter, leaving the latter near death. After his return, the scene is set for him to seek vengeance against those who acted so savagely against his family.

The story recaptures for us the ritual elements leading up to a vendetta. Melibeus summoned

> a huge multitude of men, among whom were physicians of surgery and physic, also elders and young men, as well as some neighbors, who feared rather than loved him, and some who had become friends after having been enemies and had returned to his favor. Many yes-men and flatterers gathered,

as well as wise *causidici*. And he, relating in order all that had happened to him and seeking their counsel, showed his strong desire to carry out a vendetta.[21]

The composition of this group strikes us immediately. There is no mention of relatives. Only two groups are identified by profession, physicians and *causidici*. The presence of the first is easily explained by the injuries to his wife and daughter. The latter, with the adjective *sapientes*, belong to Albertanus's own profession. Theirs is a special role in the story. The presence of the *causidici* also places the story within the context of the Italian commune. The absence of relatives of Melibeus relates to the special situation of the new urban rich and plays a significant role in the story. Against popular clamor raised in favor of swift vengeance, the *causidici* recommend the unpopular course of thoughtful delay and deliberation. They advise that due consideration be paid to the risks involved in a decision to pursue the vendetta. Theirs is the voice of the professional counselor, but at this stage their advice has little appeal to Melibeus. His wife, Prudence, however, intervenes.

What follows is a statement of the positive and negative view of vengeance and self-defense, in which the strength of Prudence's character persuades Melibeus to listen to her advice. Prudence and Melibeus discuss the value of the advice he has received, couched along lines already familiar to medieval readers. The central issue remains whether Melibeus will pursue his desire for revenge. The story builds to a dramatic climax as the reader awaits Melibeus's decision. At each step of the argument, he raises objections to the counsel offered by his wife.

While presenting a moral tale in the manner of previous moralists, Albertanus has altered the form to that of a scholastic debate concealed behind the dialogue of Melibeus and Prudence. Prudence begins by concentrating on the moral issues involved. She explores the psychology of human motivation: the role of cupidity and lust, the reasons why advice from others is so often bad. She criticizes various groups who have listened to flatterers and false friends.

Albertanus's vision of the urban experience serves as a model for this dialogue. In pointing to Melibeus's error in summoning too many counselors, Prudence discusses the way in which the deliberations of the assembly of citizens result in bad decisions if they follow "the will of the crowd rather than the wisdom of the few."[22] For Albertanus, the wisdom of the few is that of learned men, especially those of his own class and profession. He expresses this in an analogy with medicine. If Melibeus wishes to see his daughter healed he should pay the physicians well, even if they are friends. A rich reward elicits their best efforts.[23] The expert should be motivated to provide the best and his advice should be followed. The advice offered by the wise *causidici* is the kind of professional advice that Albertanus has in mind. Prudence counsels Melibeus: "This counsel is plain and correct."[24]

Even though Albertanus has now made clear the direction he is taking, he must still, through the words of Prudence, deliver a detailed argument analyzing the advice given by the wise *causidici* at the beginning of the story and carrying their deliberations to a successful conclusion. The *causidici* had counseled delay and thoughtful consideration, not attempting to deal with the heart of the matter: the reasons why Melibeus should or should not pursue his vendetta. Prudence has assumed the role of the *causidici* as she leads Melibeus toward a solution that will resolve both the moral and practical issues he faces. The story builds to its climax. Having already pointed out the direction for the solution of the problem of urban violence in a mediated settlement, Albertanus proceeds to a discussion of the practical issues and problems that must be solved first. In place of the application of moral principles that we might expect, the thrust of the dialogue is aimed at removing obstacles to a solution of the conflict through a reasoned analysis of the risk inherent in particular courses of action. Moral choices confront practical realities.

Although there has been a general tendency to regard medieval morality as derived from general ethical principles and authorities, a careful reading of Albertanus shows that this explanation has only a partial validity. Albertanus certainly valued fundamental principles, but he also valued reason as a tool in understanding morality. In a special way, the *Liber consolationis* illustrates the moral process, the way in which a choice between good and evil is made. At no point in this process does authority settle the matter. Life is viewed as a series of prudential decisions in which norms may set limits but seldom resolve the difficulties of practical existence. Necessity and utility guide the choices to be made. Albertanus does not discuss the conscience of the individual as a factor in morality, which seems rather surprising in light of his awareness of sacramental penance. His concern is not with abstract principles so much as it is with the consequences of human actions in concrete circumstances.

Since the root of conflict lies in the fact that people trust chiefly their own power, weapons, and fortifications to defend themselves from others, Albertanus works to undermine the notion that these provide a secure basis for defense. His discussion of tower fortifications illustrates the extent to which his tract draws on the experience of Italian urban life.[25] The tower was virtually a symbol of the Italian city. It brought the mentality of the feudal countryside within the walls of the town. Not surprisingly, therefore, the building of such towers was to Albertanus a visible symbol of pride on the part of the powerful that created such fear "that neighbors who had been friends became enemies." These costly fortifications, he has Prudence say, are without value "unless they are defended at much cost with help of prudent and trustworthy friends." He concludes that towers are the cause of so many evils that they should never be built save as a last resort.[26]

Such opposition is hardly surprising, but his willingness to admit an exception *is,* especially in a moral tract. His recognition that practical circumstances are important in shaping moral imperatives is, as we have seen, essential to the thought of Albertanus. He recognized the importance of defense, but suggested that other means were better because they did not carry the same threat to the order of the community.[27]

In an interesting passage, he analyzes the ties that bind groups of people together and the conflicts of interest that fragment such bonds.

> Your enemies are indeed three, but they have many children and brethren, and other relatives, and if you should kill two or three of them while pursuing the vendetta, others would remain with sufficient power to quickly destroy you. Moreover, you should know regarding your own friends, that although they are more numerous than the friends of your enemies, they are not the same as theirs; for theirs are relatives and neighbors, but yours are remote and joined in a distant relationship.[28]

The enemies of Melibeus possess numerous relatives and clients, characteristic of the landed lords of the *contado,* whose rural base of support enabled them to play leading roles in urban political life. In contrast, Melibeus appears more dependent on his urban friends and neighbors. Albertanus seems almost to be depicting the classic dilemma of the wealthy burghers confronted with the power of the nobility. But, as we know, his picture is rather over-simplified, since the nature of political alliances seldom reflected social divisions so narrowly. Nevertheless, as a statement of the differences between the social organization of the nobles and the burghers, Albertanus's analysis highlights an essential element in urban society: its instability. Though he does not pursue it, he has reached the point of seeing why city life must inevitably be founded on both a civic spirit and political institutions. This unarticulated assumption continues to influence his thought throughout the remainder of *Liber consolationis*. In a more immediate sense, it is what leads Prudence to conclude that advice in support of the vendetta is not consistent with reason, "because the right of punishment is permitted to no one save the judge having jurisdiction."[29]

This section of the tale of Melibeus concludes with a discussion of the role of law—the public right to impose penalties as opposed to the private law of the vendetta. But Melibeus rejects the advice of Prudence, arguing that tolerance of injury brings new injury.[30] Prudence responds that it is up to the judges to punish wrongs so that they do not invite new offenses by criminals. "And, therefore, such judges and podestàs should be chosen rather to investigate, to prosecute carefully, and to punish crimes and criminals than to suffer to be despised, to be cast down, and with their shame to be removed from dignity and office."[31] She continues to explore the risks involved in the vendetta, pointing out the danger in resisting the powerful and the need to proceed with patience. But Melibeus argues that such patience is a counsel of perfection and beyond his ability.[32]

He argues for his right of self-defense. But Prudence warns him that he is not immune to sin in seeking vengeance. The right of self-defense is not in agreement with the desire for revenge, since no one is allowed to act with excess in his own defense.[33] Melibeus also wishes to trust in his great wealth to overcome his enemies, even if they are stronger than he in numbers. Again, Prudence must weigh for him the proper relationship between wealth and power, warning him that he risks poverty.[34] Here Albertanus makes one of his favorite points. Wealth brings power; loss of wealth brings poverty and loss of power. Weakness before the powerful is one of the chief marks of the poor.[35] The abuse of riches leads to the abuse of power. This argument shows how riches lead to war, which may well result in their loss.[36] If Melibeus is to avoid this risk, he must avoid the vendetta. The only way to avoid war is through reconciliation.

The tale of Melibeus ends with a ritual of reconciliation that emphasizes the moral transformation of both parties to the possible vendetta. Albertanus presents a visual and spatial drama on the essential role of ritual in making concrete the fundamental change of values on which the process of reconciliation finally rests. It is a drama that moves between the secular and the sacred, incorporating elements of each. The external form is that of a treaty negotiation, in which Prudence acts as an intermediary. This merely provides a framework, however, for a sacramental change that involves a revaluation of fundamental cultural values. The process of reconciliation is complete only when the secular and sacred are unified in the final ritual.

Those who have wronged Melibeus are convinced by Prudence that they must confess their wrong. At this point, the ritual outlined follows that of a treaty negotiation. The presence of witnesses and oath-takers is an essential part of this process. Melibeus's enemies seek the advice of their friends and relatives (those, in other words, who would have participated with them in the vendetta), and ask their approval of the attempt at reconciliation. The decision is reached, but one of the group suggests a delay so that they may gather a large assembly and proceed with honor. This suggestion is rejected, but it has served to bring into the open a major stumbling block to reconciliation, namely, the role of honor in relationships within the medieval commune. Rejection of outward honor by Melibeus's enemies is given a sacramental significance as they approach him with the words "Domine, nos sumus indigni venire [Lord, we are unworthy to come]," a phrase clearly reminiscent of the "Domine, non sum dignus" of the communion of the mass.[37] At the same time secular forms are also followed. The enemies pledge to obey the commands of Melibeus with oaths and oath-helpers, and on bended knees and in tears to subject both themselves and their property to him.

But Melibeus does not immediately accept their plea. He must consider the wrong done to him and a fitting penalty. After the physicians assure him that his daughter is recovering, he tells Prudence that he intends to seize their goods and send his enemies into exile beyond the sea, a rather clear reference to the crusade as an act of penance. Prudence objects that this action is not consistent with reason.[38] She advises him to consider what this action will do to his honor. He is rich and powerful; the exacting of such a penalty is an abuse of his power. The basis for reconciliation is not divine judgment or the rigor of the law, "but rather the benignity of peace and concord."[39] Clemency, mercy, and piety form the basis for reconciliation. To exact punishment would merely exacerbate the situation and lead to the very result that must be avoided: the vendetta.

Prudence has appealed to that very concept, honor, that lay at the root of the vendetta. But she has infused it with new meaning drawn from both secular and religious sources. She concedes and even emphasizes the importance of honor and a good reputation, only to argue that Melibeus's enemies have honored him by placing themselves in his power and that he will bring shame upon himself by punishing them as he proposes. His concern for his honor would lead to an abuse of his power and ultimately to the vendetta itself.

It is apparent that the way through this impasse involves a fundamental change on the part of Melibeus as well as his enemies. They must begin to see the social relationships within a framework that is dramatically different from that which led to the vendetta. The fundamental nature of that transformation is noted by Melibeus himself, when, having relented and accepted the road to reconciliation, he addresses his former enemies who now beg forgiveness on bended knees. "Your sweet words and soft answers have quelled our anger and indignation. . . . In addition, too, your devotion and contrition of heart, and penitence and confession of sin have persuaded us to be appeased and to show our mercy and piety." And so he received them "in the kiss of peace."[40] This image of sacramental reconciliation confirms the depth of the moral transformation needed, in Albertanus's mind, to bring about a reformation of his urban microcosm. The ritual of reconciliation thus combines both secular and sacred elements, making evident the relationship between practical morality and the necessity for fundamental change in societal values. This man of law seems to be telling us that in the crisis of his society the law was not sufficient of itself to bring about so essential a change as that needed to end the vendetta.

Restored to the urban context of the thirteenth-century commune in Italy, the tale of Melibeus provides dramatic insight into the causes of factionalism and the sources of conflict that constantly threatened the peace of the cities. Disparity in power, rank, and wealth emerges as the most potent factor in promoting disorder. The dangers of the vendetta form the backdrop of urban existence. Albertanus identifies with those who worked to transform the traditional values that had entered the city from the countryside and posed such dangers to urban life. He draws on his own personal experience and observations in his search for answers. What we witness in this tract, as in his other writings, is the foundation of that civic spirit that would flourish in Italy and provide a new moral context to European cultural and political life.

Notes

1. Milan, Archivio di Stato, Fondi religiosi, S. Cosmo e Damiano, Cart. 65 (13 August 1249). See also Marta Ferrari, "Intorno ad alcuni sermone inediti di

Albertano da Brescia," *Atti del istituto veneto di scienze, lettere ed arti* 109 (1950–51): 74. The reference to Albertanus as a notary in the document of 13 August 1249 is unclear because of the form of the name: "ut continetur in una carta atestata MCCXXXVI facta per Albertanus de Porta."

2. *LP* 19:677, 687.

3. Sundby, *Liber,* 127. "Explicit Liber Consolationis et Consilii, quem Albertanus, Causidicus Brixiensis, De ora Sanctae Agathae, compilavit atque composuit sub anno Domini M°CC°XL°VI° in mensibus Aprilis et Maii." See page 1 for the dedication to his son, John, and the latter's profession of surgery.

4. This concept was studied extensively in Ernst H. Kantorowicz, *The King's Two Bodies: A Study of Medieval Political Theology* (Princeton, 1957). The approach taken by Albertanus would suggest a somewhat different development.

5. See for example the interesting discussion in Brian Tierney, *Religion, Law, and the Growth of Constitutional Thought, 1150–1650* (Cambridge, 1983), 37–38.

6. On Mattheus of Correggia, *LP* 19:598–602; Pressutti 2:242(4960), 271(5114); *MGH Ep.* 1:189–90. For the citation from Rolandinus, *RISS,* n.s. 8:1, 5.

7. The calculations given in this paragraph are based on the citations in Sundby's edition of the *Liber consolationis* and those in his edition of the *De doctrina* compared with those in Hiltz's dissertation. (Sharon Hiltz, "*De amore et dilectione Dei et Proximi et aliarum rerum et de forma vita:* An Edition" [Ph.D. diss., University of Pennsylvania, 1980].) They may not be totally accurate, but they do provide an adequate basis for the conclusion reached here.

8. Sundby, *Liber,* 12–20.

9. Ibid., 12; Sharon Hiltz, "*De amore,*" 119–27.

10. Boethius, *The Consolation of Philosophy* (Cambridge, Mass., 1946), 3, 6.

11. Sundby, *Liber,* 90.

12. Boethius, *Consolation,* 4, 7.

13. Godofredus Prior, *Epigrammata, RS* 59:2, 127. Godofredus is also referred to as Pseudo-Martial because of his extensive reliance on the writings of the Roman poet. Albertanus habitually cites him as Martialis Cocus. See Hiltz, "*De amore,*" 331, for references.

14. Godofredus, *RS* 59:2, 111.

15. Hiltz, "*De amore,*" 90–91.

16. Publius Virgilius Maro, *The Georgics and Eclogues of Vergil* (Cambridge, Mass., 1915), "Eclogue 1."

17. John W. Baldwin, *Masters, Princes, and Merchants: The Social Views of Peter the Chanter and his Circle,* 2 vols. (Princeton, 1970) 1:261–311, has thrown important light on this Parisian literature.

18. Lester Little, *Religious Poverty and the Profit Economy in Medieval Europe* (Ithaca, 1978), 173–217, esp. 200.

19. *Sermones quattuor,* 30. "Et liberare debemus pro posse pauperes a potentibus." Cf. Psalm 71:12. (Vulgate) Also, Sundby, *Liber,* 98–99. "Per temporales insuper opes et divitias acquirit homo magnam potentiam. . . . Et nota quod, sicut occasione opum temporalium atque divitiarum praedicta bona et infinita alia consequimur, ita amissis opibus atque divitiis paupertatem atque indigentiam et

necessitatem incurrimus, atque omnia mala sustinere cogimur." The same view is expressed in the Hiltz, *"De Amore,"* 158.

20. Ibid., 212.

21. Sundby, *Liber,* 6.

22. Ibid., 65–66. "Inde est, quod in partitis, quae in consiliis civitatum fieri consueverunt, consilium semper malum sortiuntur effectum, et non paucorum sapientium, sectantur."

23. Ibid., 67.

24. Ibid., 68–69.

25. Ibid., 72–73. "Munitio turrium et [aliorum] altorum aedificiorum ad superbiam plerumque pertinet, et timor et odium inde generatur, ita quod vicini et amici propter timorem fiunt inimici, et omnia mala inde nascuntur, quae occasione timoris notavi tibi supra in titulo: De Vitando Consilio Illorum, qui non Amore, sed Timore Reverentiam ostendunt. Quare Salomon dixit: 'Qui altam facit domum suam quaerit ruinam; et qui evitat discere, incidet in mala.' Praeterea turres cum magno labore et infinitis expensis fiunt; et etiam cum factae fuerint, nihil salent, nisi cum auxilio prudentium et fidelium amicorum et cum magnis expensis defendantur." Vatican City, BAV, Vat. Lat. 991 om. aliorum; vicini *et* amici.

26. Ibid., 74. "meo arbitrio nunquam turres sunt faciendae, nisi tunc demum quando aliae munitiones deficiunt vel non sufficiunt."

27. Ibid., 74–75. "Munitio multiplex est. Est enim munitio, quae ad dilectionem pertinent, ut amor civium; et hoc inexpugnabilis est. Est alia munitio, quae roborat animam et corpus, videlicet, virtus; et haec similiter inexpugnabilis est." These are stronger than material fortifications in Albertanus's view.

28. Ibid., 78. This passage is a very clear statement of the nature of social bonds in thirteenth-century society: "Inimici vero tui sunt tres, multos habent filios et germanos et alios necessarios, quorum si vindictam faciendo duos vel tres occideris, alii remanerent, qui personam tuam cito destruere valerent. Circa illos alios tuos amicos notare debes quod, licet multo plures sint quam inimicorum amici, tamen non sunt tales ut sui; nam sui sunt necessarii et propinqui, tui vero sunt remoti et longinqua parentela conjuncti. Ita circa illos, qui consentiunt tibi vel illis, et circa principales personas, illorum conditio valde melior est quam tua." Vat. Lat. 991 om. *valde.*

29. Ibid., 78. Here Albertanus uses the terminology of the law: "Et certe non est [vindicta] consentaneum rationi, quia de jure vindicta nulli nisi judici jurisdictionem habenti permittitur." Note the use of *vindicta* in both technical and popular meanings in this passage.

30. Ibid., 91.

31. Ibid., 91–92. "Tales itaque judices et potestates potius eligantur, maleficia et malefactores investigare, sollicite insequi atque punire, quam patiantur ab eis contempni et deici atque cum suo vituperio a dignitate et officio removeri." Vat. Lat. 991 has *eligantur* where Sundby has *eligant.*

32. Sundby, *Liber,* 95–96.

33. Ibid., 95–96.

34. Ibid., 98.

35. *Sermones quattuor,* 25.

36. Sundby, *Liber*, 101–2.

37. Ibid., 113–18. "Illi vero respondentes dixerunt: Domine, nos sumus indigni venire ad curiam tanti et talis domini. . . . "

38. Ibid., 119.

39. Ibid., 122. " . . . sed hic non debet tractari de judicio divino nec de juris rigore, sed potius de pacis et concordiae benignitate."

40. Ibid., 126. "Insuper etiam vestra devotio cordisque contritio et poenitentia atque peccati confessio nos induxerunt ad placabilitatem, clementiam et pietatem." For the relationship between the secular and the sacred, see also Guido Ruggiero, *Violence in Early Renaissance Venice* (New Brunswick, N.J., 1980), 1–2.

5. *Congregatio Nostra:* The Role of the Confraternity in the Formation of the Professional

THE LAST YEARS of Albertanus's life were divided between his public service and his participation in the confraternity of *causidici* in Brescia. Although the manuscript tradition has often separated Albertanus's treatises from his sermons, at least to the extent that there are many more manuscripts of the former than of the latter, we have already seen that the *De doctrina* and the *Liber consolationis* reflected his professional interests and his views on the transformation of society as much as his sermons did.[1] The relationship of the individual to the community that stood at the heart of the *De amore* is central to the sermons he delivered to the Brescian *causidici*. His vision of voluntary submission to a rule, which provided the structure of the *De amore,* applied very specifically to the organization of his profession. Confraternity lay at the foundation of his conception of the meaning of profession, which he spells out in detail in the sermons he delivered at this time. The quasi-priestly role that he assigned to his fellow professionals was strengthened through their membership in a confraternity. Judges and *causidici* were bound by the highest ethical standards. They were instruments not merely for the preservation of order in society but also for bringing about reform through both their personal and professional activities. Their rule, or *propositum,* was a microcosm of that which Albertanus had spelled out in the *De amore.* While much in these sermons relates directly to Albertanus's earlier writings, it is evident that they stand apart as a kind of summary of his views on his profession.

Although we cannot be certain, it seems likely that all of these sermons were delivered around 1250 in the church of San Giorgio Martire, which was then entrusted to the Friars Minor.[2] The Franciscans had come to Brescia about the time that Albertanus was beginning his writing career. Little is known of this early phase of their history. They were certainly not as prominent in the religious life of the city as the Dominicans, evidenced by the fact that the first Dominican prior in the city, Guala, became bishop in 1229 and retained that position until his death in 1243.[3] Nevertheless, the Franciscans were well respected and admired. In 1254, the commune undertook the construction of a new and larger church and convent, the present San Francesco, to serve their needs. Interestingly, it was located not far from the church and quarter of Santa Agata.[4] But it was in the church of San Giorgio Martire that Albertanus and his fellow *causidici* were accustomed to gather for their meetings and their banquets, often in the presence of one or more of the friars.

The early history of confraternities in northern Italy remains obscure.[5] Most of the evidence dates at the earliest from the late thirteenth century. The publication of statutes from neighboring Bergamo by Lester Little has shed some light on activities in Brescia, as has the study of the Humiliati in Brescia.[6] However, a note of caution is needed. The meeting of the confraternity of Brescian *causidici* in a Franciscan Church does not suggest an embryonic Third Order, or lay fraternity associated with the friars. The earliest evidence for the Third Order in Brescia dates only from the period after 1289 and the first membership list is from the opening years of the fourteenth century.[7] A study of that list does not reveal participation by any of the leading families of the city. On the other hand, the confraternity of *causidici*, if not prestigious, probably enrolled several members of leading families if the active members of the profession around 1250 were members.

Of the dozen *causidici*, including Albertanus, listed as active in Brescia between 1225 and 1254, several have names prominent in the public life of the city. Conradus de Bagnolo appears in a document of 10 June 1232. He is related to a large and important family that included Zilius de Bagnolo, a judge, and Gerardus de Bagnolo, who had served as a consul in 1173.[8] Johannes de Turbiado is mentioned in the same charter.[9] His family played a leading role in the politics of Brescia in the thirteenth century. As in the case of the Bagnolo, other members of the Turbiado are mentioned in the documents of the period. Stephanus de Turbiado was a consul in 1219.[10] Otto Villani, who appears as a *causidicus* in 1251, was in all probability related to Petrus Villanus, who had served not merely as a judge but also as an ambassador of the commune.[11] But most *causidici* were not from such prominent families. Some, like Crescimbenus de Prato Alboyno and Gracius de Yse, from Iseo, may have served in the rural areas outside the city and been members of substantial local families, but it is uncertain how often they were in Brescia or whether they participated in the confraternity.[12] However, most of those named in documents from the late 1230s through the early 1250s were probably members of the confraternity.

The importance of a professional confraternity in the Italian commune cannot be overemphasized. In a society torn by violence, membership in such groups reinforced efforts to establish an orderly society. More importantly, but less stressed in recent writings on the topic, the ethical standards established for the members played a critical role in shaping professional life. It is precisely this area that the sermons of Albertanus provide specific evidence to support that already found in his other writings. The moral dimension of professional development was essential to the creation of an effective body that could serve the total needs of society. We have already seen how Albertanus stressed the importance of service to the poor without remuneration. In his sermons, we get a more complete picture of his views concerning the nature of professional service.

Albertanus's first Brescian sermon examines the rule of the confraternity. "Gathered here in our accustomed manner, we examine the rule of our congregation, treating some useful matters concerning it."[13] We learn about the meetings of the members, how they were accustomed to gather, possibly in the evening since Albertanus mentions that "oil is purchased from which this sacred place is illuminated."[14] One feature of the meeting was the spiritual refreshment, "which we are accustomed to receive with devotion from the friars here." This reference makes it clear that this sermon was delivered at San Giorgio, in the presence not only of the members of the confraternity but also of one or more members of the Franciscan community. The meeting also included a meal. Albertanus discusses each of these aspects of the meeting and applies them to the professional lives of the members.

The three undated sermons in the Brescian collection form part of a series, bound by a common theme enunciated in the first sermon. Together they form an extended commentary on the *propositum* of the confraternity of *causidici* at Brescia in the mid thirteenth century. Indeed, they would appear to be the only extant commentary on such a rule by a layman.[15] The fourth and final sermon, dated mid-Lent 1250, may be read as a climax or conclusion to this series, thereby establishing the date and circumstances for their delivery. This sermon sums up the meaning that Albertanus gave to his profession, a fact that gives it a special significance in the history of professional confraternities. These sermons taken together form an important treatise, connecting Albertanus's professional concerns to his religious life and his ideas about the reform of society.

The first sermon announces his intention to treat some "useful mat-ters" concerning the rule, beginning with the concept of light: "it is im-portant that those who wish to show their light to others should have light within themselves."[16] Albertanus builds upon the image of the oil lamp, which gives light to the meeting of the confraternity. "In order to confer true light on others, it must be known that, just as in our usual corporeal light we need four things, namely, fire and oil and a pure vessel in which the oil is poured and can be burned, and the burning itself, so also in the spiritual light we need these four things." Fire represents the warmth of love. Moreover it consumes sins.[17] It is the image of Pentecost, of Moses and the burning bush, of the column of fire that led the Jewish people through the desert. It is the image of the coals heaped upon the head of one's enemy.[18] Oil is the "splendor of good works and the works of char-ity." Albertanus relates the parable of the ten virgins, five of whom were prudent and five foolish. He stresses the purity of the oil; we ought not to do acts of charity out of vanity. God does not forget works of charity, but on the day of judgment He will say, "I was hungry and you gave me to eat; I thirsted and you gave me to drink; I was naked and you covered me; I was a stranger and you sheltered me; I was ill and in jail and you visited me."[19] Albertanus adds that works of this kind should not be done un-willingly or under duress, but joyfully. Just as material oil is for illumi-nation, for warming food, and for anointing, so spiritual oil, the oil of charity, leads us to the true light. It is pure, reflecting the purity of our intentions, as our bodies should be pure.

Albertanus stressed light as an illumination that shines from the soul of the person engaged in good works. We must remove all impediments that would extinguish our light, as wind and air extinguish the flame of the lamp.[20] Without obstacles, light will be everywhere diffused.[21] This diffusion of light has particular significance both for the professional ac-tivities of the *causidici* and for the transformation of society as a whole. The pursuit of happiness, the *beata vita*, discussed in the *De amore*, is approached in these sermons from a different point of view, that of the role of judges and other urban legal professionals in making such happi-ness possible. The diffusion of their light is the fulfillment of the respon-sibility that had already received so much attention in Albertanus's writings. We meet here a statement of the relationship between the con-fraternity of the *causidici* and the world at large. These sermons resemble the *De amore* in that they are a commentary on a rule, but they are directed to a particular professional group.

In the last section of his first sermon as well as in his two following sermons, Albertanus takes up the theme of spiritual and corporal refreshment. His discussion of spiritual refreshment is interesting not merely for what it says, but for what it does not say. He relies heavily on texts used to describe the sacrament of the Eucharist as spiritual food. He speaks of the bread of angels and the "living bread," which is Christ. He quotes from the Lord's prayer a passage which has often referred to the Eucharist: "Give us this day our daily bread."[22] He also speaks of the "wine of compunction for our sins."[23] But his concept of spiritual refreshment serves chiefly to introduce the subject of corporal refreshment.

Recent studies have shown the importance of food shortages in helping to shape the medieval attitude toward food and fasting. A direct relationship existed between the hunger of the poor and the idea of fasting. The poor were the beneficiaries of the surplus created in this way.[24] Regulations about food played an important role in all religious rules, including those of the Orders of Penance. A statute of a confraternity of penitents from 1215 was typical in its rules about abstinence from meat and fasting.[25] It fixed the usual exceptions for the weak, infirm, and travellers. It enjoined moderation on all of its members. Similar regulations are found in the *Memoriale propositi* dating from the 1220s.[26] They are also to be found in Gratian's *Decretum*.[27] In most of these sources, there are also prohibitions of "inhonesta convivia," banquets at which improper entertainment is offered.[28] Albertanus was clearly aware of this tradition. In fact, he presents his own views on food, particularly on provision for the poor, drawing partly on the *Decretum*. But he differs from the traditional views in significant ways. Much of what he says is conventional enough. He begins by quoting the following ditty:

Sit timor in dapibus, benedictio, lectio, tempus,
sermo brevis, vultus hilaris, pars detur egenis.

[At banquets, let there be fear, a blessing, a reading, time, a short sermon, a happy face, a share for the needy.][29]

It serves as a basis for his remarks.

Fear operates as a restraint on overeating. A blessing commences the meal. Next comes a reading. Albertanus draws directly on Gratian's *Decretum* by observing that "religious observe this practice [reading] as well as waiting for the third sacred hour, before [going] into the banquets [*con-vivia*]."[30] A brief sermon follows. Albertanus says that "we ought to have a happy face"; and, finally, that a share should be given to the needy. Here he uses *egeni* rather than *pauperi* to stress physical over spiritual poverty.

Again he gives a verse about the four things that must be avoided at the banquet. "Pleasures, slander, drunkenness, grumbling should be avoided." And, he explains, "Pleasures should be avoided. For we ought not desire pleasures and delicate foods, though we can use them if they are taken without any desire."[31] It was a view commonly applied not merely to food but to sexual pleasure as well. Albertanus criticizes those who complain about food and drink, or drink too much. He accepts the monastic view that "we ought not care about the quality of food." He praises moderation and emphasizes care for one's health.

These views are entirely consistent with those expressed in the confraternity rules discussed above, but they avoid specifics about fasting and abstinence, taking their inspiration from the *Decretum*'s regulations aimed at the clergy rather than from the statutes of lay confraternities. The extent to which his views were shaped by canon law is indicated by the manner in which he ends this discussion by quoting from the decree, "Non liceat," which was also to be found in the *Capitula* of Martin of Braga.[32] This would suggest that the rule or *propositum* of the confraternity of *causidici* was little influenced by the rules of the Order of Penance.

Albertanus's second sermon deals with spiritual refreshment, especially the practice of charity and alms-giving toward the needy and the poor. Taking his text from Psalm 40:1 ("Blessed is he who is concerned for the poor; God will free him on the evil day"), he explores the various meanings of terms referring to poverty in order to understand them.[33] The "needy" are those who "are in need of some necessities." The poor are so called from the fact that they have little. The "poor in spirit" are separated from those who are "poor in the substance of this world." To these he adds yet another category, the *inopes*, the helpless who are without resources, defined as those without power.[34] This latter group figures significantly in Albertanus's thinking on the issue of poverty. They stand in contrast to the *potentes*, who combine wealth and power, and from whom the poor must be liberated.[35] Having classified the types of poor, and having put particular stress on the idea of helplessness in a way that was unusual in medieval thinking about poverty, Albertanus goes on to analyze "how we ought to understand the needy and the poor."[36] He organizes this investigation according to the seven principal senses: the two "senses of the soul," intellect and affection; and the five bodily senses, sight, hearing, taste, smell, and touch.

This approach, which may seem artificial, corresponds closely to the medieval approach to the poor. Poverty had both a spiritual and material dimension. It was not enough to care for bodily needs; it was also important to understand the value of the poor as human beings and the religious significance of attitudes and actions in behalf of the poor.[37] Albertanus presses the need for good understanding and good intention in the service of the poor as well as "good will, great affection, and joyfulness."[38] He condemns the notion that one should aid the poor as a result of pressure. "Forced service does not please God."[39] He continues with an analogy to the five bodily senses. Sight involves both the eyes of the body and the eyes of the mind or the heart. He reproves those who turn their eyes and face away from the poor. Even when the poor are absent, they should be present in heart and mind. "We should listen to their cries and not harden our hearts." Taste refers to eating, especially to the breaking of bread together.[40] Albertanus treats smell allegorically, referring it to prayer, which like incense gives off a good odor to people and returns a good odor to God. But prayer also had a special meaning for the *causidici* to whom this sermon is addressed. For they ought to pray for the poor and needy, that is, to plead for them without charge before those presiding over their trials, before the rich, the consuls of justice, and others having jurisdiction. If the *causidici* plead in the cases of the rich for money, the more easily should they plead in the cases of God or the poor for eternal life.[41] Finally, Albertanus's treatment of the relationship between touching and understanding the poor and needy reminds us of the attitude of his contemporary, Saint Francis of Assisi, toward the leper. Albertanus actually cites the example of Jesus cleansing the leper by touching him.[42]

Care for the poor arises not merely from religious obligation or intellectual conviction, but from direct knowledge through the bodily senses. Albertanus stresses the physical reality of poverty in a way that has been ignored in some modern scholarship.[43] The difference in his approach highlights the degree to which other medieval sources tended to emphasize the spiritual value of poverty over its physical reality. Certainly, this approach was deeply rooted in the monastic tradition. Albertanus, however, shows a much greater affinity to those who identified with the great mass of the suffering poor than to a religious ideal of poverty. In this dimension, his thought is closer to the radical trends found in the twelfth-century poverty movement.

The remainder of this second Brescian sermon is given over to practical issues about helping the poor that must reflect debate in the more affluent circles of urban Italy. First, Albertanus disposes of the argument that some lack the means to help the poor. Lack of money is no excuse in his eyes, for there is always, "prayer, good will, and compassion."[44] Secondly, he deals with the argument that the giving of alms does not benefit spiritually a giver who is in mortal sin. This argument, though not put into a particular context, raises the question whether those involved in usury were not prone to neglect charity on these grounds. Albertanus responds, "Certainly it is true that such alms do not profit as to perfection, still alms given out of charity profit, even while someone is in mortal sin."[45] He argues that they profit one's good name and reduce punishment, on the ground that no good goes unrewarded—an interesting point in terms of the church's teaching on sin and merit. He also maintains that alms lead to increased riches in this world, taking the classic line that the Lord rewards those who give.

Wealth is not decreased but increased and grows as a result of giving. In support of this view, Albertanus gives the example of Jesus feeding the multitude with loaves and fishes. But he also maintains that "we can recognize that human riches are not diminished by alms through many human examples. For we have seen many good houses, whose riches grew abundant and increased when they were generous in giving alms, but when, through greed, alms ceased, the goods of those houses were totally destroyed."[46] He also argues against those who say that they wish to leave their money to their relatives. The idea that God will reward those who are generous to the poor in this world was commonly accepted, but Albertanus seems to want to go further in asserting a natural phenomenon along the same lines. While this argument is in line with his usual attempt to support his case with examples drawn from reason, it also suggests that he had some insight into the way in which distribution of wealth could stimulate economic growth. He seems almost to be arguing that support for the poor is an investment. If this is the case, it represents a rare insight indeed. Given other observations that he makes regarding investment and income, however, it does not seem entirely farfetched.

Since the Lord has left the poor to their care, the *causidici* must be their refuge and help them in their tribulations. "We ought to liberate the poor, if possible, from the powerful." This image, reminiscent of modern liberation theology, was deeply rooted in the theology of Christianity. It shows the complexity of the issues of poverty in contrast to the arguments of those scholars who have viewed medieval concern for the poor in terms of preserving the established order. Albertanus was not a revolutionary in any sense; he sought to build an orderly society. But the dominance of the powerful over the poor was to him an aberration, destructive of the stable order that he sought. He wanted to redress a serious imbalance in society. "We ought to rise up to their help because of their misery. . . . If the poor take anything from us, we should spare them because of their poverty."[47] He piles reason upon reason to argue in favor of support for the poor, summing up finally that "the reasons are infinite."

After dealing with the rewards for almsgiving, he says "And this is notable and more than notable, that almsgiving is the highest good [*summum bonum*] in man."[48] With this, he returns to the beatitudes, concluding "if therefore the giving or denial of alms is the reason why God will give or deny eternal life to us, we ought to care for the needy and the poor with such solicitude that we may be blessed and, in the evil day he will free us and say to us: 'Come, blessed of my father, receive the kingdom.'" The second sermon was, therefore, a powerful commentary on the nature of poverty and the obligation of the confraternity to give alms to the poor.

Such an emphasis was unusual in the religious rules for the laity. Though we sometimes find references to providing for those in need among members of the association, as in the *Memoriale propositi,* and encouragement of works of piety, as in the rule of the Poor Catholics of 1208, in both of these cases what was contemplated was corporate charity, undertaken under the auspices of society.[49] Albertanus put much more stress on the action of individuals. While he refers to the feeding of the poor at the meal of the confraternity, he views this action in symbolic terms. Care for the poor is a responsibility of each member of the group. The confraternity, in his view, is directed toward reform of the individual.

Albertanus focuses his third sermon on the banquet or *convivium,* that is, on bodily refreshment. In his treatment of food in the first sermon to the Brescian *causidici,* he relied on Gratian's *Decretum.*[50] In the present sermon, his emphasis is no longer on food but on the social meaning of the *convivium.* This is clear from the definition that Albertanus gives that "*Convivium* is the coming together in friendship of the good, but dissension among the evil."[51] This quotation from a certain philosopher, as Albertanus calls him, alerts us to the theme of the sermon. First, Albertanus deals with preparation for the *convivium*. He says that not everyone should be invited, only the good and the poor.[52] He congratulates his fellow *causidici* because they have invited "istos pauperes Minores ad convivium vestrum," that is, they have invited Friars Minor to share their repast. With his usual fondness for puns, he quotes the Gospel of Saint Matthew: "Quamdiu uni ex minimis meis fecistis, et michi fecistis [As long as you have done this for the least of my brothers, you have done it for me]." The friars gathered there must have been delighted by this flattering reference.

In this sermon, he continues to emphasize the theme of caring for the poor that he developed in his second sermon. In fact, he deliberately reminds his listeners and readers of that theme, by quoting again, "Beatus, qui intelligit super egenum et pauperem: in die mala liberabit eum Deus [Blessed is he who is concerned for the needy and the poor; God will free him in the evil day]," employing the text that he had used in his second sermon.[53] In the final portion of this section, he treats those things needed for preparation for the *convivium*: spiritual foods, bodily foods, and mixed foods, "which profit both body and soul."[54] These categories are reminiscent of those we have already met in his first sermon referring to spiritual and bodily refreshment.[55] Now they refer to food, and a new category of mixed foods has been added. At this point, he reveals that his own sermon will be followed by one by a Franciscan friar, who "will speak after me and will feed us with spiritual food."[56] After this brief introduction, he moves on to emphasize "mixed foods," which he defines as "speech, truth, justice, judgments, through which judgment ought to be exercised." His chief concern is with the professional qualifications of those engaged in judicial work, that is, those like himself who are judges and *causidici*.

The relationship of this sermon to the *De doctrina dicendi et tacendi* emerges immediately from Albertanus's reference to the treatise: "Therefore I have spoken as I could about how the tongue should be controlled, because no one can completely control his tongue," and he cites the verse from the Epistle of Saint James with which he had begun that treatise.[57] It thus serves to demonstrate the unity of his thought. Further, his conception of rule, which had its origins in the *De amore*, has found expression once again in the idea of the rule of the confraternity. The ethical significance of speech, which we have traced throughout Albertanus's writings, is now developed as it meets the needs of a confraternity of urban professionals, the *causidici*. The microcosm of the professional reflects the macrocosm of society; the macrocosm informs the microcosm. The relationship between the individual, his membership in a profession, and society as a whole takes on a deeper meaning as result of a continuing process of extrapolation of these various roles.

The importance of controlling the tongue, of putting a brake on speech, as well as the emphasis on the value of silence, take on a professional meaning that was present in the *De doctrina* but finds its most complete application in this sermon. Without going over ground already covered, we can easily note that not only do the same bits of advice reappear, but the fundamental structure of the presentation remains very much the same. The relationship of this sermon to the Genoese sermon, which was itself a prelude to the *De doctrina*, is also evident.[58] As the third Brescian sermon continues, its professional meaning becomes more and more evident from the emphasis it puts on judgment. Albertanus explores those things which are necessary for judgment: "Knowledge, jurisdiction, reason, deliberation, justice, fear of the Lord, and necessity."[59] He stresses the responsibility of the judge to "prepare justice." One observation strikes a sympathetic note to the modern ear: "For there is such a confusion of laws, decrees, and decretals, that the memory of man is hardly sufficient for judging. Wherefore the law says: 'To retain the memory of everything and to err in nothing is rather divine than human.'"[60]

Albertanus's discussion of judgment provides interesting insights into the approach of practicing judges in the early thirteenth century. He maintains that necessity rather than will should be a major element in judgment. The judge must avoid being influenced by his own will in rendering judgments; it is not a surface impression but a just judgment that must shape judicial decisions. Likewise, in swearing oaths, necessity and utility should determine whether or not an oath should be taken. Albertanus cites the example of the mendicants, Dominicans and Franciscans, both strongly committed to poverty, who add to their churches and houses as needed, to illustrate the overriding importance of necessity and utility in reaching decisions. Necessity and utility are fundamental to making moral choices. They supplant other considerations, especially those based solely on will or desire. Albertanus also stresses the expertise and knowledge needed in reaching a judgment.

He refutes those heretics who deny the validity of judgments, saying "bodily punishment rests with the Lord alone."[61] In so doing, he distinguishes between the religious, that is, members of religious orders, and those living in the world. The religious are bound to accept injustices and to turn the other cheek, but those remaining in the world, "even the good," follow the law that "proclaims that one can repel force with force" and whoever "acts out of concern for the protection of his body does right."[62] He cites the Old Testament acceptance of corporal punishment and condemns heretics who reject its teaching.

His stress on the heretical nature of the opposition to corporal punishment ignores the fact that similar positions were taken by orthodox Christians. His concern for order in society, his judicial experience, and his strong sense of right combine to persuade him to support corporal punishment and the death penalty. So strong is this feeling that he ends his sermon with the story of the good thief on the cross next to Christ, using it to justify the death penalty.[63] He argues that "otherwise, there would be so many criminals who would steal the clothes and food of good people that no one good could live." It is a sentiment that has echoed through the centuries. That it should appear so strongly in the writings of Albertanus illustrates the strength of his commitment to professional legal procedures and law as the way in which society could achieve happiness and prosperity. He is a realist who recognizes on numerous occasions the flaws and imperfections in the legal system and those who administer it, but does not allow that to deter him from supporting it and trying to improve it.

It is therefore not at all surprising that his final sermon returns to a view of the *causidici* he had referred to earlier in the *Liber consolationis et consilii,* that of the *causidici* as wise counselors.[64] Now he says, "My dearest brothers, you are called wise by men, you should take care by the highest effort . . . that you may be wise, and may possess true wisdom."[65] Thus he has returned to the essential element of the legal profession. Without wisdom, all other procedures lose their meaning. For Albertanus, this wisdom is grounded in "fear of the Lord." Aside from its religious and theological significance, which is of course fundamental, it is evident that the idea of fear of the Lord has for Albertanus a profound psychological meaning. Fear of the Lord removes other fears, "namely human, mundane, servile, and all things will fear us." This fear also reduces the need for worldly goods, and hence the temptation to accept bribes often offered to judges. Fear of the Lord makes judges free. "We acquire not only liberty, but also the highest freedom."[66] Thus there is a measure of confidence and independence granted to those who fear the Lord. This quality, so obviously lacking in the existing conditions described by Albertanus, was essential to the development of the judicial profession. In his view, it proceeds from a religious source. Fear of the Lord leads to happiness and to the perfect good, which is "the true wisdom and the knowledge of divine and human affairs. . . . For the highest comfort in life is the study of wisdom, and he who finds it is happy and he who possesses it is blessed."[67]

For Albertanus, wisdom is a struggle: "We ought to bear the arms of justice against all evils while we are thinking." Judges must not be corrupted by friends or neighbors or the powerful. "And, if perhaps our friend should insist, desiring us to withdraw from a good *propositum* to an evil one, we should have the constancy and keep in mind the saying of the Apostle, who said in the epistle to the Romans: 'Don't conquer by evil, but conquer evil in the good.'"[68] Judges must not commit sins for their friends and ought not to defend others in their sins, lest they "prepare a crime for themselves." These strictures are of course common in the legal literature of the thirteenth century. But they are here part of a structure of professional ethics developed within the context of an early thirteenth-century judicial confraternity. They are to my knowledge the earliest evidence we possess of the internal professional life of members of such a confraternity. It is indeed on this professional note that Albertanus ends this final sermon. Emphasizing the importance of reputation, he goes on to say that

> I have seen in my times, and I have exercised this profession for more than twenty-four years, that all who have had the reputation for justice and goodness have an abundance of good things, but the malicious, who have a reputation for injustice and evil-doing, have almost all been destroyed with all their substance and all their goods, and rightly so.[69]

It is to this end that Albertanus directs his profession: "so that our name may be of consequence for affairs and we may be truly wise . . . and may avail to ascend to the kingdom of God."[70]

From this series of sermons, we get a picture of the meaning of membership in a confraternity of professional men in early thirteenth-century Brescia, and perhaps in northern Italy as well. Despite the attendance of Franciscans at the meeting, the relationship to the friars was informal and chiefly indicative of the kind of work in which they were engaged in the mid thirteenth century rather than evidence of a formal relationship. It is not surprising to find them working with an association of Brescian *causidici*. We cannot learn much about the extent of their influence from the sermons. It would be nice, for example, to argue that Albertanus's ideas paralleled those of the early friars, but we cannot be certain that this was the case. Even his outspoken support for the poor need not be tied to the Franciscans, since the early rule of the Third Order more nearly resembles other rules for the laity than the positions outlined by Albertanus. But the degree to which he was committed to the concerns of his profession and its moral needs suggests that he and his fellow *causidici* had little interest in either the Orders of Penance or the more radical groups of penitents.

Albertanus's view of heretics confirms this conclusion. For him the confraternity of *causidici*, the wise *causidici*, had an exalted role to play in society. They had the obligation to promote order and social harmony. Their work was fundamental to the building of a better society. Albertanus viewed heresy almost entirely from the perspective of its destructive impact on society. Heretics challenged the authority that was essential to the performance of the judges' societal function.[71] Albertanus did not condemn them for their theological errors or for their rejection of ecclesiastical authority, points usually emphasized in contemporary ecclesiastical writings on heresy, but for their rejection of the right of secular authority to mete out corporal punishment and the death penalty. As we have seen, neither of these views was heretical and both could be found among some pious groups of orthodox believers. Albertanus based his view not on a religious foundation but on a position frequently taken by leaders of the communes.

The *propositum* projected by the study of these sermons owes little to the early rules of the Order of Penance collected by Gérard G. Meerssemann.[72] It is of a different type, though not uninfluenced by the spiritual currents of the twelfth century that also spawned these rules. On the one hand, it harkened to a long-established tradition of professional associations that had its roots in the early Middle Ages but flourished especially in this period. On the other, it was the expression of a new professionalism that played such an important part in the political, social, and economic life of the Italian cities in the twelfth and thirteenth centuries. Albertanus captured this spirit and attempted to fit its pieces into a meaningful pattern. He had already begun to think about this prior to his composition of the *De amore* in 1238. But he had not yet focused completely on the nature of his profession and its societal role. That only emerged gradually in the Genoese sermon and in the *De doctrina*. By the time he came to write the Brescian sermons, Albertanus was able to focus his thought on the needs of his fellow *causidici*. To these wise men he entrusted the future happiness of mankind. Where previously he had hinted at a special role for them—an almost sacred role—he now assumed that they were practitioners of wisdom in behalf of society.

These sermons do not supplant what he had written earlier. Indeed, the idea of *propositum* unites these sermons to the *De amore* and, ultimately, to his other writings, a point made clear as we examine their interrelations. In Albertanus, we see a thinker struggling to work out a solution to basic societal problems on both a theoretical and practical level, in terms of an overarching idea that would subsume the organization of society into the conception of a voluntary rule. It is all too easy to show the inadequacies of his works in both their theoretical and practical aspects. But the same may be said for many if not most later systems. For there can be no doubt that Albertanus was a systematizer. He deserves recognition for his great originality and creativity in pointing the way toward a restructuring of society in which the idea of community was balanced by the voluntary choice of the individual.

Notes

1. In the thirteenth century, the sermons seem to have appeared in conjunction with the treatises about half the time. Among the best examples are Vatican City, BAV, Vat. Lat. 991, which contains all of the treatises and the five sermons; Milan, Biblioteca Ambrosiana, B. 40 Sup.; and Cambridge, Gonville and Caius College, 61 (155). In the fourteenth century, however, manuscripts without the sermons outnumber those with the sermons by two to one. See Appendix.

2. Cinzio Violante, "La chiesa bresciana dall'inizio del secolo XIII al dominio veneto," *Storia di Brescia* 1:1064-1124, esp. 1077.

3. Ibid. 1:1076–77. The Franciscans arrived in the 1220s and took up residence at the church of San Giorgio Martire.

4. Ibid. 1:1077. The new church was constructed by the commune to celebrate the victory over Ezzolino da Romano.

5. The best introduction to confraternities in Italy is found in Monti, *Le Confraternite medievali dell'alta e media Italia*. 2 vols. (Venice, 1927), updated by articles in Meersseman's *Ordo fraternitatis*. For recent literature, see Lester Little, *Liberty, Charity, Fraternity: Lay Religious Confraternities in Bergamo in the Age of the Commune* (Bergamo, 1988).

6. Violante, "La chicsa bresciana" 1:1078–81. Little, *Liberty*, 17–97.

7. Violante, "La chicsa bresciana," 1:1084; Paolo Guerrini, "Gli statuti di un'antica congregazione francescana di Brescia," *Archivum franciscanum historicum* 1 (1908): 544–68; John R. H. Moorman, *A History of the Franciscan Order from its Origins to the Year 1517*, 218–19; Gérard G. Meersseman, "Il manuale dei penitenti di Brescia," *Ordo Fraternitatis* 1:410–50, esp. 450.

8. *LP* 19:417.

9. Ibid. 19:417, 566.

10. Ibid. 19:114.

11. Ibid. 19:699; for Petrus Villanus, 19:46, 61, 627.

12. Ibid. 19:417, 841.

13. *Sermones quattuor*, 3–15. "More solito hic congregati, propositum nostre congregationis inspiciamus, circa illud aliqua utilia pertractantes."

14. Ibid., 3.

15. I do not consider the *Cedrus* of Boncompagna da Signa a commentary. Gérard G. Meersseman, "Per la storiografia delle confraternite nel medioevo," *Ordo Fraternitatis* 1:3–34, esp. 18–22.

16. *Sermones quattuor*, 3. For discussion of the liturgy of illumination, see Jacques Chiffoleau, "Entre le religieux et la politique: Les confréries du Saint-Ésprit en Provence et en comtat Venaissin à la fin du moyen âge," in *Le mouvement confraternel au moyen âge* (Geneva, 1987), 19–24.

17. *Sermones quattuor*, 3.

18. Ibid., 4.

19. Ibid., 4–5.

20. Ibid., 8.

21. Ibid., 9.

22. Ibid., 10–11.

23. Ibid., 11.

24. Michel Mollat, *The Poor in the Middle Ages* (New Haven, 1986), 49; Carolyn Walker Bynum, *Holy Feast and Holy Fast* (Berkeley, Cal., 1987), 33–41.

25. Meersseman, *Dossier*, 88.

26. Ibid., 95–98.

27. *Decretum*, D, 42, 1.

28. Meersseman, *Dossier*, 281, 293.

29. *Sermones quattuor*, 12.

30. Ibid.; *Decretum*, D, 44. In vol. one of *Corpus Juris Canonici*, ed. Emil Friedberg, 2 vols (Graz, 1959).

31. *Sermones quattuor*, 13.

32. *Decretum*, D, 44, 12. *Corpus Juris Canonici* (Friedberg), 1, xxii, has the reference to the *Capitula*.

33. *Sermones quattuor*, 19; Psalm, 40:1.

34. *Sermones quattuor*, 20.

35. Ibid., 30.

36. Ibid., 20.

37. Mollat, *Poor*, 1–11.

38. *Sermones quattuor*, 20–21.

39. Ibid., 21.

40. Ibid., 22–24.

41. Ibid., 25.

42. Ibid.

43. Richard C. Trexler, "Charity and the Defence of Urban Elites in the Italian Communes," in *The Rich, the Well-Born, and the Powerful*, ed. Frederick C. Jaher (Urbana, Ill., 1973), 64–109 presents another view.

44. *Sermones quattuor*, 26.

45. Ibid., 28.

46. Ibid., 29.

47. Ibid., 31.

48. Ibid. 33.

49. Meersseman, *Dossier,* 103, 287.

50. *Decretum,* D, 40, 44.

51. *Sermones quattuor,* 37.

52. Ibid., 38.

53. Ibid., 19. See note 33.

54. *Sermones quattuor,* 39.

55. Ibid., 3.

56. Ibid., 39.

57. Ibid., 40; Sundby, *De doctrina,* 479.

58. *Sermones quattuor,* 45–46; see text in *Sermone inedito di Albertano, guidice di Brescia,* ed. Luigi F. Fè d'Ostiani (Brescia, 1874), 44–45.

59. *Sermones quattuor,* 46.

60. Ibid., 47–48.

61. Ibid., 48–49.

62. Ibid., 50.

63. Ibid., 52.

64. Sundby, *Liber consolationis,* 8.

65. *Sermones quattuor,* 57.

66. Ibid., 59.

67. Ibid., 60.

68. Ibid., 61–62.

69. Ibid., 63.

70. Ibid., 63–64.

71. Ibid., 50–51.

72. See Meersseman, *Dossier,* passim, and notes 25, 49.

6. The Causes of Violence

THE BREADTH OF ALBERTANUS'S VISION of social reform has emerged with greater clarity from a study of the structure of his writings. The pattern formed by the underlying unity of his thought has eluded those who have focused on the moral arguments that form threads within the total fabric. But even though we have succeeded in casting considerable light on the underlying purposes of Albertanus's writings, something more remains to be done. The chief question asks whether Albertanus's abilities as a synthetic thinker were matched in any way by his critical capacities. Was he able to move beyond the attitudes and explanations found in his sources to attain an understanding based on an analysis of fundamental problems in his own society? Does his writing represent merely a rehash of traditional advice delivered with platitudinous voice to his sons and colleagues, or does he try to fashion answers to questions about the real sicknesses of his society? The problem is greater than it might seem, since presumption favors the former rather than the latter response.

The formulation of a coherent body of theory and its application to a particular society was a rare undertaking in the early thirteenth century. We have already mentioned how Albertanus's efforts differed from his contemporaries, the Bolognese *dictatores* and the authors of the podestà literature. We have also described his writings against the background of the Senecan tradition. If Albertanus was not a typical product of his age, he was nevertheless very much at home in a period profoundly involved in the great issues of human existence. For Albertanus, man of the commune that he was, the issue of violence loomed above all others. If he on the one hand desired to reconstruct society along more peaceful and orderly lines, he also wanted to explain the causes of those disorders that needed remedy. His ties to his own profession gave him practical insights; the writings of past moralists gave him reasons and words. But the structure of his solutions and the analysis of the problems were to a major degree his own.

The concept of rule provided Albertanus a framework for his ideas about society and the relationship between society and the legal profession. He distinguished rule from law. For him, the notion of rule was more fundamental than law. Rule represented an underlying consensus on which law was ultimately founded. Without the voluntary acceptance of rule, there was no possibility of a society bound by law. For Albertanus, law was limited in its capacity to resolve the problems of society by the necessity of a previous conversion by those submitting to it. They must willingly give up some part of their individuality to participate in the action of the community. Albertanus did not posit a natural-law foundation for human law. Instead, he seems to have worked from a notion of human consensus based on the voluntary acceptance of a rule. This consensus provided a social fabric within which human law functioned. Behind it stood the wisdom of the past, which for Albertanus informed human reason. His was a far different picture from that which emerged from studies of Aristotle in the second half of the thirteenth century. Aristotelianism went much further than Albertanus in establishing boundaries between the human and the divine. The increasing importance of natural law theory in the second half of the century opened the way to more rigidly hierarchical structures than those implied in Albertanus's consensus theory. Under his concept of rule, the distilled experience of the ancient world, whether from the pagan classics or the Bible, laid a basis for a rational understanding of human moral conduct.

Reason played a major role in shaping Albertanus's view of moral judgment. His use of both classical and biblical sources aimed not so much at settling moral questions in a definitive way as in providing a framework for further discussion. He seems to have been moving toward a methodology of moral decision-making. Even in taking positions bolstered by traditional arguments, such as the right of self-defense or just war, or the defense of the death penalty, his arguments were not merely summaries of previous authorities. His use of citations was structured in such a way that it depended not merely on the authority of the text but also on the reasonableness of the argument. The notion of "rule" as the foundation for Albertanus's systemization of his social thought is therefore not a simple matter of specific regulations of human behavior, but the acceptance of a rich tradition of human experience based upon both pagan classical and biblical texts that provided a structure for moral philosophy.

In dealing with his fellow professionals, Albertanus took his conception of "rule" from the *propositum* of the confraternity. But he was not limited by the traditional forms of confraternity rules. His extensive commentary on the *propositum* of the confraternity of *causidici* in his sermons went beyond the usual limits of such rules. It applied ideas he had already developed for society as a whole to the specific role of a dedicated group, that is, one sharing a common purpose and function within society and for this reason in need of a "common" rule. While directed to the needs of members of his own legal profession, his writings were not limited to the needs of one profession. Rather, they are applicable to the roles of all professionals within the larger society.

What is particularly interesting is the high degree of social responsibility built into Albertanus's conception of a profession. A profession is not merely a group bound by a common body of knowledge and particular skills, but also one whose practice should conform to certain moral standards. His criticisms of those who violate those standards leaves no doubt that he regarded morality as an essential element in the making of a profession. This view seems to lie behind one of his most personal comments:

> And I have seen this in my own times, having served in this profession for more than twenty-four years. For I have seen that all having the reputation for justice and goodness abound in all goods, but I have seen that almost all the malicious, having a reputation for injustice and evil behavior, have been destroyed with all their substance and all their goods, and with merit. And who are these evil men? They are those who use their professional knowledge and skills solely for their own profit.[1]

Despite his strong belief in the reforming role of the legal profession, Albertanus seems to have been particularly aware of the problems attendant on assigning such responsibilities to a particular group. If we might suggest that there were Platonic or Stoic tendencies in his approach, it becomes evident after a more thorough reading of his treatises that he did not share Plato's ideas about the rule of philosopher-kings. Not only did he assign the legal profession a more limited role, but he constantly pointed to the risks of corruption that hindered its effectiveness. His view of the role of the legal profession was further restricted by his conception of the part played by the law itself. As we have noted above, Albertanus recognized that law could only be effective to the degree that it was accepted by society. Even coercion and punishment had to occur within the context of a societal commitment. The insight represented in these ideas is all the more significant if we consider it in the light of his sources. Although his view certainly reflects attitudes we find in Seneca,

Albertanus has dropped entirely the pessimistic strain that marked the Roman philosopher's writings and adopted a more positive approach to the possibility of social reform. The isolation from the community that marked the Roman is almost totally absent in Albertanus. Reform of the individual, which was central to Seneca's thought, has become a social act symbolized in the Christian concept of conversion with its connotations of participation in a community.

Along with consideration of this theoretical structure, which extends to the manner in which Albertanus organized his works and dealt with practical moral *dicta*, we need also consider the relationship between his ideas and the society in which he lived. Albertanus was rare in his capacity to surmount the limitations of his life in Brescia in order to achieve a deeper understanding of the problems that troubled the lives of ordinary people. But he was not a closet scholar; he was intimately involved both as a professional and through his work in the confraternity of *causidici* in trying to bring about the changes he advocated. This aspect of his activity is particularly illustrated by his role as a lay preacher.

Medieval lay preaching has not yet received the attention that it deserves, despite the pioneering work by Gérard Meersseman and the increasing interest of others.[2] In particular, we know little of such preaching in the twelfth and thirteenth centuries. Most of what is known relates specifically to the approval by the papacy of preaching by former Waldensians and Humiliati. Unfortunately, these studies have tended to encourage the view that lay preaching was often tinged with heresy and was the product of groups deeply influenced by the movement of apostolic poverty. Thus the two major figures cited by Meersseman as exemplars of such preaching in the thirteenth century, Francis of Assisi and Rainerio Fasani, both had ties to the development of the Order of Penance.

While it is evident that Albertanus was influenced to some degree by the Order of Penance and some of his views reflect attitudes common to those who embraced the movement of apostolic poverty, he was much more clearly identified with a tradition of lay preaching that was associated with professional confraternities. In fact, as Meersseman has shown, lay preaching enjoyed a long history within the western church, reaching back to apostolic times.[3] While the twelfth century did witness increasing concern over heretical preachers, modern scholarship has unduly emphasized this aspect of the development of lay preaching. Actually, much heretical preaching was the work of clergy, particularly disaffected members of the lower clergy. There is no evidence in the sermons of Albertanus that he saw his position as unusual, or that he was speaking with the permission of the clergy. Nevertheless, as Meersseman has pointed out, his topics lay within the sphere of moral preaching and his sermons emphasized conversion.[4] For the most part he avoided questions of doctrine. The only extensive passage of a doctrinal nature deals with the elements in the sacrament of penance, which, as we have seen, were part of his approach to the resolution of the vendetta.[5]

We have already noted a distinction in his treatment of religious topics between his treatises and his sermons. This difference should not be exaggerated; it reflects more the particular context of the writings than a real difference in character. In both his treatises and sermons, Albertanus approached moral issues from a perspective that reflected reason more than revelation. Moreover, his religious perspective possessed a civic character that fit into his communal outlook. The authority and institutions of the church remain very much in the background of his writings. Despite his criticisms of clerical shortcomings in one passage, he tended to be quite sympathetic to institutional problems, as is evident in the way in which he spoke of the Franciscans and the Dominicans.[6] He wrote confidently about moral issues and supported religious values, but he spoke always as a layman. Civic goals were his main concern, civic morality his chief topic, and to the extent that he dealt with religion, it was religion as a civic force underpinning society.

Already in the *De amore*, Albertanus tried to give coherence to his ideas. That alone makes it a good place to start. The *De amore* begins with the love of God and continues by exploring the nature of the closest human relationships, those among friends, neighbors, and family. This consumes the first two books. Book 3, which deals with the love of material things, discusses relationships between work and leisure as well as wealth and poverty. It treats of war and its consequences, and the forms of the vendetta, both public and private. In his final book, Albertanus takes up virtues and vices, concluding with a section on conversion to the Lord and on the choice of the active and contemplative life. From the outset, it is apparent that certain topics were of special concern to Albertanus. His relationship to wife and family occupied a very important place in his thinking, as is evident not only in the *De amore* but also in the dedications of his other treatises and in his discussion of wife and family in the *Liber consolationis*.[7]

War, violence, and the vendetta form another principal theme that runs through much of his writing. This topic is closely tied to his concerns about his own profession, which we have already shown to occupy a paramount position in his structuring of his ideas. War and violence are also connected to his views on wealth and poverty. Thus there is a considerable coherence to his treatments of all these subjects. Finally, Albertanus directed all of his writing toward ways in which the tensions that produced injustice and conflict in society could be resolved.

Since we have already dealt with the religious aspects of Albertanus's thought, the remainder of this chapter will treat his ideas about society. For the purpose of this study, it is not important to distinguish on each and every occasion whether Albertanus was speaking his own words or quoting from another; it is sufficient that he has given a final structure and meaning to the ideas whether his own or borrowed. When he decided to copy the words of Cicero or Seneca or a text from the Old Testament, these quotations ceased to be the exclusive property of their authors and took on new meaning and context from the way in which Albertanus used them. We must read them as a part of his argument, as presenting his reasons or illustrating his points. Unless we are able to do this, we stand to lose much of his meaning.

In the *De amore,* the concept of friendship expresses the relationship between different kinds of persons without regard even to class.[8] Within the family, friendship is important in defining behavior, but it is even more important outside of the family circle. Proceeding from love of God to love of neighbor in the classic Christian manner, Albertanus subjects love and friendship to an intensive examination of the perils that threaten human relations. His second book looks at those who abuse or misuse the love that is offered them. He begins by examining depraved love, in which the senses move out of control.[9] The love of fools must be avoided because they recognize the vices of others but not their own. "Nor can you even speak harmoniously with a fool: for he does not pay attention to anyone's reason, nor give a hearing to anyone; so if you speak to him, you lose your words."[10] Likewise, the friendship of greedy men should be avoided. Avarice is not limited to the rich; it does not matter "whether you lie sick on a wooden bed or one of gold."[11]

While no single Italian commune can serve as a model of the varied communal experience of northern Italy, Brescia and its neighbors did undergo many problems that affected towns and cities in other parts of Italy. Divisions of commune and *contado,* of rich and poor, and the predominance of violence in town and countryside were a shared experience, no matter how local circumstances might influence behavior in different ways. For Albertanus, as we have seen, the problem of violence was central. Not surprisingly, much of his writing was an attempt either to explain violence or to find solutions for it. While his explanations for violence are not entirely original, there is considerable originality in the way in which he links violence to economic disparities. Power in the hands of the rich and powerful lies at the root of violence, because they seek to get their wills by force.

This situation graphically describes the social tensions in Brescia in the early thirteenth century.[12] Albertanus draws on his own experience. He contrasts the *potentes* and the *pauperes* in his thinking. But he does not make a simple dialectical division between rich and poor; rather the division is between those with power and those without power. The question of wealth is secondary. This emphasis on power rather than wealth explains how Albertanus could adopt a positive attitude toward riches while condemning the actions of powerful men.[13] In the *Liber consolationis,* Melibeus is rich, but he lacks power because he lacks those strong family connections and ties of patronage or lordship that would enable him to overcome his enemies. In contrast to him, his enemies have large families and many dependents and friends to support them.[14]

The division between *potentes* and *pauperes* lay at the root of violence. But in order to understand Albertanus's views on the problem, we must first examine his understanding of poverty. Recent literature on poverty in the Middle Ages has a strong tendency to contrast the medieval attitudes toward poverty with those that developed in the fifteenth and sixteenth centuries.[15] But a careful study of Albertanus shows that such a division is overly simple. Most of the attitudes that exist in the later period were already present in his thought. Succinctly put, he was influenced by the way in which poverty affected the fabric of society. He was of course concerned about the needy and devoted much of his writing to traditional expressions about caring for and feeding the poor. Especially in his sermons, we find that he encouraged alms giving and the practice of charity as outlined by Christ in the Gospel of Saint Matthew:[16] "For I was hungry and you gave me to eat; I was thirsty and you gave me to drink; I was naked, and you covered me; I was a stranger and you sheltered me, sick and imprisoned and you visited me." He follows this statement with a classic Catholic view on the value of almsgiving, saying that Christ did not say, "'Because you were sober, chaste, humble, devout, continent, meek, or you did such good things,' but only rendering account of almsgiving, he says: 'For I was hungry and you gave me to eat, etc.'"[17] The very fact that Albertanus mentions these attitudes toward the poor confirms how commonly they were held. In the past, too much attention has been paid to a supposed contrast between medieval and modern views of poverty. What Albertanus makes clear for us is the diversity of attitudes toward poverty among members of the thirteenth-century professional and middle classes.

He strengthens his position by quoting, "We ought to, if possible, free the poor from the powerful [Et liberare debemus pro posse pauperes a potentibus]." This statement is itself based on a quotation from Psalm 71:12: "He freed the poor from the powerful, the poor man, who had no helper."[18] In the *De amore*, Albertanus says that "we cannot be equal to the powerful."[19] But this should not be read as a counsel of despair. Albertanus is merely summing up realistically the relationship between the weak and the powerful. Implied in this statement is his view that the powerful cannot be overcome by individuals, even such wealthy persons as a Melibeus, but only by society and its rules, guided by legal professionals. His concern for the freedom of the individual from the wealthy and powerful is reflected in his statement "You should not barter your liberty by taking a dishonorable or unworthy gift."[20] Throughout his writings, Albertanus argues that wealth is both necessary and desirable, but it must be used properly. As we have seen, he even argues that the mendicants share his attitude in their own use of money to add to their churches and convents as needed.

Poverty was a social crime, the source of many inequities. Albertanus has no praise for indigence. Rather, he criticizes its existence. He argues that the able-bodied should work to support themselves instead of depending on charity.[21] Jacques LeGoff has recognized that Albertanus has a distinctive place in the history of medieval work because he gave "the value of labor, considered more as a skill than as toil," his top priority. LeGoff therefore adds another objection to the thesis advanced by Max Weber, who argued that the ideological promotion of labor was a fruit of the Protestant ethic.[22] But Albertanus has done much more. He views poverty and labor within the framework of a social theory that perceives the relationship between them. He not only distinguishes, as his contemporaries did, the types of poverty, but he sees in poverty a root of the injustice that imperiled social order. The care of the poor for Albertanus goes beyond the giving of alms; it is a function of preserving the social order.

> Through temporal wealth and riches, man acquires great power, so that kings and princes and most other men seek and fear it. And note that, just as we obtain the aforementioned goods and an infinity of other things because of temporal wealth and riches, so with their loss, we incur poverty, indigence and need, and are forced to bear all evils.[23]

Albertanus is not referring to poverty in a spiritual sense or to voluntary poverty in this passage. He recognizes the spiritual value of poverty, but argues that men must avoid "evil" poverty.[24] "You should avoid poverty that leads to need and indigence."[25] For him, "need is the mother of crimes."[26] He thereby emphasizes the social impact of poverty, bolstering his arguments with appropriate quotations from Cassiodorus, Seneca, and Petrus Alfonsi.[27] Here we are far removed from the often romanticized view of Franciscan poverty symbolized by Saint Francis's embrace of Lady Poverty. That was the embracing of voluntary poverty, the adoption of an attitude toward poverty based on rejection of worldly goods. It referred to the spirit of poverty rather than to the social evil as described by Albertanus. When he speaks of the liberation of the poor, it is the destructive effects of indigency, the impotence of the poor before the powerful, that he has in mind.

At root, Albertanus's concern about wealth and poverty is closely connected to his analysis of the causes of violence. We can best understand his approach if we turn to the first chapter of this book in which we discussed the roots of violence in thirteenth-century Brescia. In order to understand his perspective, we must realize that he shared the viewpoint of those who suffered most from the conflicts among the powerful. He was demonstrating how the poor were victims in the conflicts among the rich and powerful. They were caught in the interstices of violence. As dependents, they had no choice but to rally around their wealthy protectors. Their tragedy was that they lacked the freedom to follow their own wills. The source of violence lay in the behavior of the rich and powerful. This is the quintessential message of the *Liber consolationis*. It is a tale of a vendetta involving powerful lords within one town, with their fortified towers and hoards of relatives, friends, and dependents. But it is also an effort to understand the nature of violence and to show how it might be brought to an end. Not surprisingly, Albertanus saw violence in intensely personal terms; it reflected personal wrongs, and was exemplified in family relations.

The family stands at the heart of Albertanus's theory of society. For him, the ties of family are essential elements in all other human relationships. It is to the family that a person must turn for essential support in time of need. This is the lesson of the *Liber consolationis*. Melibeus not only finds his best advice in his family, in the person of his wife, but she tells him about the importance of family in maintaining social status.[28] While the *De amore* laid down guidelines for the relationship between a father and his children and man and wife, the *Liber consolationis* probes the meaning of family relationships in society.[29]

Prudence, the wife of Melibeus, is more than the personification of an abstract virtue; she stands for the female principle. Albertanus makes this point by summing up the negative and positive images of women according to the well-established tradition in medieval literature.[30] He begins by discussing why a husband could not take advice from his wife. In the *De amore,* he wrote, "Although you ought to love your wife, you should not give her power or primacy over you, because she may not agree with you."[31] He gives the same reason in the *Liber consolationis.*[32] But in the latter, he also presents arguments from the opposite side, or as he entitles them, *De excusatione mulierum* [On the excusing of women]. This approach achieved considerable popularity in the later Middle Ages.[33] Writing in the late fifteenth century, the anonymous author of the Florentine *Fior di virtù* explained this technique:

> I am determined to defend [women] against anyone who wants to speak badly of them. I shall therefore proceed as follows: First I shall quote the authority of certain wise men who speak kindly of women, then the authority of those who speak ill. And finally I want to compare these sayings, giving a truthful declaration and absolution, cutting the vile tongue of the perverse talkers as they deserve it.[34]

The author of the *Fior di virtù* resolves the seeming conflict by arguing that those who speak ill of women "refer to bad women."[35] He concludes:

> In fact every day, we see examples of women strongly resisting and defending themselves against the violence of men, while the latter do not have to defend themselves against women. So that those who speak so badly of these poor and unfortunate women would do better to be silent since, naturally, they do not have a true and honorable foundation.[36]

This same bad woman/good woman motif appears in the argument presented by Prudence against Melibeus: "You have said that all women are so evil that no good woman is found. . . . There are infinite good women."[37] In fact, very likely Albertanus influenced the discussion in the *Fior di virtù,* as we may see from the following passages:

> *Liber Consolationis*
> And it is no objection that Solomon said: "I have not found a good woman," because even if he did not find one, many others have found good women.
> *Fior di Virtù.*
> Nor does the authority of Solomon contradict me when he says that he has never found a good woman, for if he has never found one, there are many who have and one cannot deny that there have been good women before and after him.[38]

For Albertanus, the validity of the advice offered Melibeus by Prudence forms an important part of his argument in favor of women. He has made Prudence the wife of Melibeus, the mother of his daughter who lies critically injured throughout this discussion. Prudence speaks to him not merely in the guise of an abstract virtue but as a wife to her husband. She uses the classic argument that woman is man's helper, made such by God. "And well can women be called helper and thus as a result counsel, for without the help and counsel of women the world could not endure."[39] Albertanus cites Seneca, who commended "kind wives."[40]

Albertanus makes it clear that while he regards the husband as a generally dominant figure, he believes that wives are partners rather than mere subordinates. Prudence concludes her discussion by quoting from the *Sententiae* of Publilius Syrus: "The chaste matron rules by obeying her husband."[41] And her own words show precisely this quality: "If you wish, therefore, to direct yourself prudently and with my advice, I will bring your daughter, God willing, to health and will help you get out of this affair with your honor."[42] Her use of the word "prudently" [*prudenter*] seems hardly accidental given Albertanus's liking for word-play and puns. It reinforces the positive argument about the role of women that he has been presenting. This positive attitude toward women is also found in other passages in his writings. For example, he advises his sons to marry not for money but because of the grace and virtues of their fiancées.[43] He strongly opposes heretical views on marriage that condemn sexual acts as inherently evil. But he does defend the traditional position on male rights in marriage.[44] On the whole, however, he portrays marriage and the relationship between man and wife in a balanced fashion.

This picture is completely in harmony with Albertanus's vision of society. All of his writings make clear that he desired to promote peaceful resolution of conflict within the family and in society as a whole. He regarded this goal as a special function of the members of his own profession, but he was fully aware of the difficulty in achieving the end he desired. His view of violence was based on the idea that every effort should be expended to prevent it. If that proved impossible, violence should at least be limited and controlled. Above all, the use of coercive force should be reserved to those holding public office and exercising power in the name of the community to carry out whatever actions were needed to restore peace.[45] Albertanus opposed "heretical" rejections of the right of self-defense, just war, and the death penalty, all of which he defended as proper functions of government.[46] They were necessary in defense of the rights of the community and the individual. He only reluctantly endorsed these means, however. They were last resorts. There is a risk that some may overlook his reluctance, failing to see that for Albertanus the road to a better society lay along a different path than the way of coercion.

Particularly in the *Liber consolationis* but also in the *De amore*, Albertanus strove to show the perils of submitting decisions to violent solutions. As Prudence warned, "The fortification of towers and high buildings quite often is a sign of pride and it generates fear and hate, so that neighbors and friends become enemies out of fear."[47] Fortifications are very expensive and are of little value. Albertanus in the *De amore* argues that "If someone is poor, in no way can he support a war; if, however, he is very rich, his expenses will increase the more."[48] Wealth is lost through war. Also, to fight against the powerful is dangerous.[49]

His approach to the vendetta argued against the use of force. While admitting the lawfulness of self-defense, Prudence cautions Melibeus again and again against the risks involved. She describes the power of his enemies and his own weakness. She stresses the risk that he would lose his wealth. Thus many arguments previously used by Albertanus against warfare were repeated in his attack on the vendetta. Albertanus stressed that the only way to reach a decision was to submit the matter to the judge having jurisdiction or to the advice of wise counselors. The final resolution of the tale of Melibeus is a triumph of peaceful means over violence.[50] The concepts of conversion and penance, so central to the religious life, are applied to society as a whole, thereby offering a peaceful end to the quest for the happiness that Albertanus saw as the purpose of human society.

Notes

1. *Sermones quattuor,* 62–63.

2. For our period, the most valuable introduction is still Gérard G. Meersseman's article on lay preaching, "Predicatori laici nelle confraternite medievali," *Ordo Fraternitatis* 3 : 1273–89. The volumes by Little, Banker, and Black, along with the older survey by Monti, are helpful. Lester Little, *Liberty, Charity, Fraternity: Lay Religious Confraternities in Bergamo in the Age of the Commune* (Bergamo, 1988); Little, *Religious Poverty and the Profit Economy in Medieval Europe* (Ithaca, 1978); James R. Banker, *Death in the Community: Memorialization and Confraternities in an Italian Commune in the Late Middle Ages* (Athens, Ga., 1988); Christopher Black, *Italian Confraternities in the Sixteenth Century* (Cambridge, 1989); Gennaro M. Monti, *Le confraternite medievali dell'alta e media Italia,* 2 vols. (Venice, 1927).

3. Meersseman, "Predicatori laici" 3 : 1273.

4. Ibid. 1 : 1287–88.

5. Sundby, *Liber,* 126.

6. *Sermones quattuor,* 48; Sharon Hiltz, "*De amore et dilectione Dei et proximi et aliarum rerum et de forma vita:* An Edition" (Ph.D. diss. University of Pennsylvania, 1980), 221.

7. Sundby, *Liber,* 12–20.

8. Hiltz, "*De amore,*" 40–156.

9. Ibid., 56.

10. Ibid., 57.

11. Ibid., 63.

12. Ibid., 68.

13. Sundby, *Liber,* 97–99.

14. Ibid., 76–78.

15. Michel Mollat, *The Poor in the Middle Ages* (New Haven, 1986), 295–300, reflects recent uncertainties about this problem.

16. *Sermones quattuor,* 33–34.

17. Ibid.

18. Ibid.

19. Hiltz, "*De amore,*" 76.

20. Ibid., 147.

21. *Sermones quattuor,* 14; Sundby, *Liber,* 99–102.

22. *Letteratura italiana. Il letterato e le istituzioni,* ed. A. A. Rosa (Turin, 1982) 1 : 660–61.

23. Sundby, *Liber,* 98–99.

24. *Sermones quattuor,* 14.

25. Sundby, *Liber,* 97.

26. Ibid., 99.

27. Ibid., 99.

28. Ibid., 18–20, 77–78.

29. Ibid., 77–78.

30. J. Verdon, "Le fonti per una storia della donna in occidente," in *Donna nel medioevo: Aspetti culturali e di vita quotidiana,* ed. Maria de Matteis (Bologna, 1986), 175–223. See esp. Angela M. Lucas, *Women in the Middle Ages* (New York, 1983), 105–34.

31. Hiltz, "*De amore*," 125.

32. Sundby, *Liber,* 12.

33. Ibid., 13.

34. *The Florentine Fior di Virtù of 1491,* trans. Nicholas Fersin (Washington, D.C., 1953), 15.

35. Ibid., 17.

36. Ibid., 18.

37. Sundby, *Liber,* 14.

38. *The Florentine Fior di Virtù,* 17; Sundby, *Liber,* 14–15.

39. Sundby, *Liber,* 18.

40. Ibid., 18.

41. Ibid., 19.

42. Ibid., 19.

43. Hiltz, "*De amore*," 123.

44. Ibid.

45. Sundby, *Liber,* 86–89.

46. Hiltz, "*De amore*," 215.

47. Sundby, *Liber,* 72–73.

48. Hiltz, "*De amore*," 196–97.

49. Ibid., 199.

50. Sundby, *Liber,* 125–26.

7. Afterlife: The Varied Influences of Albertanus's Writings

ALBERTANUS RANKS AMONG THE MOST POPULAR of all medieval writers not only in the number of manuscripts of his writings that have survived but also in the number of authors who have drawn on his work in significant ways. In addition, between the thirteenth and the sixteenth centuries numerous translations of his works appeared in Italian, French, German, Spanish, Dutch, and Czech, while printed editions of his works abounded from the fifteenth century on.[1] To some degree, interest in his writings continued even into the seventeenth century, though on a much reduced scale. Despite this vast reputation, Albertanus has not been accorded high marks as an original thinker, certainly not as one who helped to shape the ideas of the Renaissance and the early modern period. Paradoxically, both the assessment of his popularity and the judgment on his influence are substantially correct.

It remains in this chapter to describe how the major thrust of Albertanus's work, which we have described in preceding chapters, was altered and lost. Or perhaps it may be better to say that it was lost insofar as there could be hope in tracing specific lines of development from Albertanus to important figures in modern thought. That is not to say that such links do not exist, merely that they are, at least for now, unproven.

Writing in the first half of the eighteenth century, the great Italian antiquarian and reformer Lodovico Muratori might well have had the texts of Albertanus's works close at hand when he wrote his *Pubblica felicità*.[2] The introduction to this important essay on civil reform echoes much of the spirit of Albertanus's writings, not least when Muratori rejects the politics of power and reason of state and founds civil authority on tacit agreement of the people. Lockean as these ideas may seem, they are also in the tradition to which Albertanus of Brescia belonged. Their mention here serves merely to suggest the breadth and depth of thought on which an eighteenth-century Italian reformer might have drawn. The communal tradition was a rich well of social and political ideas that continued to nourish, even amid the adversities of the fifteenth and sixteenth centuries, major aspects of Western thought. But if figures like Macchiavelli and Guicciardini knew Albertanus, as they very well might have, it was in another context from that for which their own writings are chiefly known. The echoes in the writings of Muratori are just that.

Although we have already suggested one reason why Albertanus had less influence on political and social theory than on literary figures by exploring the relation of his thought to the major currents of the twelfth and thirteenth centuries, it is valuable to pursue other aspects of this development in the period from the thirteenth to the sixteenth century. This investigation will shed some light on the way in which Albertanus's ideas grew in some gardens and withered or died in others. One of the earliest and most important lines may be found in the popularity of his writings among Italians with strong ties to France and French culture.

The earliest translations of his treatises into Italian vernaculars came within the first generation after his death. In 1268, Andrea da Grosseto made a translation into Tuscan in Paris.[3] It was an elegant and generally accurate rendering of the original, destined to find its way into both manuscript and printed editions. A decade later, Soffredi del Grathia of Pistoia, who often accompanied Italian merchants to Provence, prepared a translation of at least one of Albertanus's treatises during a stay in that region.[4] This relationship to France was solidified by Brunetto Latini, the distinguished Florentine notary and master of rhetoric, teacher of Dante, who incorporated parts of the *De doctrina dicendi et tacendi* into his vast compendium *Livres dou Tresor,* introducing Albertanus, though unnamed, to a French audience for the first time.[5] The significance of this early French influence will become more apparent when we discuss the fourteenth and fifteenth centuries. But we must first sketch the development of Albertanus's fame and influence in his native Italy.

In some ways, the growth of Albertanus's popularity in Italy must be contrasted with what happened later to his work elsewhere, for in its native soil it seems to have come closest to being nurtured in a climate that valued its original meanings. The reason for this lies in the fact that there was no sharp division in Italy between civic culture and civil behavior as marked the thought and literature of northern Europe.[6] Even in Castiglione, such distinctions are blurred. From the thirteenth through the fifteenth century, the writings of Albertanus maintained their popularity in both humanistic and non-humanistic circles. Latin and vernacular manuscripts were produced in significant numbers. Indeed, one of the most notable is a fine fifteenth-century Vatican manuscript in a humanistic hand. Vatican Palatina MS. 403 is in Latin, luxuriously decorated with marginal floral designs, initials, and quotation marks.[7] Like other Latin manuscripts of Albertanus's treatises of Italian provenance, it seems to follow the original with only minor variations. Although few of the vernacular manuscripts are of the quality of this manuscript, they too tend to reflect the completeness and accuracy of the Latin manuscript tradition, though there are variations among the various translations, and in at least one case the translation is little more than an epitome.[8] If we can single out one characteristic of the Italian manuscript tradition, therefore, it is its fidelity to the text of Albertanus. However, despite the continuing popularity of Albertanus's works in Italy as evidenced by the continued production of manuscripts in the fourteenth and fifteenth centuries, it was the French tie that was responsible for his influence on Italian writers.

The key figure was of course Brunetto Latini, who probably introduced Dante to Albertanus. Aldo Checchini has suggested that Albertanus's influence was evident in what he saw as Dante's use of the *De doctrina dicendi et tacendi* in the *De volgare eloquentia*.[9] Santino Caramella has found some evidence of this path of transmission in a connection between Albertanus's use of "cui dicas" and Dante's question to Brunetto Latini in *Inferno* XV, 30: "Siete voi qui, Ser Brunetto?"[10] Caramella also makes a more general argument for Albertanus as a precursor of Dante, in the course of which he points out some interesting similarities and differences in thought. Of more immediate concern to us is the probability that Brunetto's experience in France broadened his intellectual appeal to the young Dante and this same tie to French culture was evident in the writing of Albertanus. However tenuous, Albertanus is a link between the twelfth century and the age of Dante that cannot be ignored.

One of the most important works that was strongly influenced by the twelfth-century moral tradition, so strong in France, was the *Fiore di virtù*, dating from the late thirteenth or early fourteenth century and represented in numerous manuscripts. Maria Corti has devoted a lengthy article to exploring the sources and influences on the *Fiore di virtù*.[11] For our purposes, the extensive use made by the anonymous author of the works of Albertanus serves as additional evidence of the way in which his writings remained closely linked not merely to the moralistic tradition but also to a work that was itself strongly influenced by the scholasticism of the thirteenth-century French schools. In the case of Albertanus, success in Paris would seem to have been the reason why his writings flourished in thirteenth- and fourteenth-century Italy. The road from Brescia to Florence led through Paris.[12]

At the same time that Albertanus's reputation was spreading among expatriate Italians in France and thence returning to Italy, it was also growing among the French themselves. Before the end of the thirteenth century, Albertanus's treatises were translated into French. The earliest manuscript (Paris, B.N. Français, 1142) dates from this period, but there are numerous other copies, including an elegant fifteenth-century illustrated manuscript, formerly the property of Henri du Cambout, duc de Coislin, the beauty of which attests to the continued significance of the works of Albertanus.[13]

The French translator was a man of considerable insight, as we learn from a note that he has left at the end of Paris, B.N. Français, 1142. He warns his readers that this is no easy body of work and he asks them "to read and reread" for they will find more than the literal meaning in the text. Like its Italian counterparts, this translation follows the Latin text carefully.[14] Mario Roques has shown that Brunetto Latini was also responsible for a French translation not merely of that portion of the *De doctrina* that he used in the *Tresor*, but for a text that circulated separately.[15] In the fourteenth century, a French translation of the *Liber consolationis et consilii* appeared, the work of a Dominican from Poligny, Renaut de Louhans. Renaut also translated Boethius's *Consolation of Philosophy*, assuredly no coincidence. Roques has shown that Renaut completed his translation of the *Liber consolationis* in 1336 or 1337, while Burgundy was embroiled in warfare. The barons had risen against the Duke of Burgundy, their suzerain; Renaut preached in support of peace and in favor of the Duke. His translation of the *Liber consolationis* is hardly surprising under these circumstances and it shows at least some understanding of the message that underlay the *Liber consolationis*. With Renaut commences the process of adapting the *Liber consolationis* to the political, social, and cultural climate of the north.[16]

Renaut's translation was more a paraphrase and a somewhat shortened version, suppressing some sections of the original and abridging others. For example, chapters six to ten on the nature of prudence, chapter 34 on pride, chapter 38 on the fivefold will of God, and chapter 48 on the cases when men can licitly fight were all omitted. Roques has also detailed significant changes in annotation, especially the omission of authors' names. Renaut also added citations from the Gospels, which Albertanus had used sparingly in the original, and some from the lives of the saints, to which Albertanus had not referred at all. The effect of these changes was to serve better the purpose of Renaut by heightening drama and directing its message of peace more immediately to the warring French nobility.[17]

About this same time, or a bit later, another development occurred in France that affected the future of the *Liber consolationis:* "It became an edifying treatise for women."[18] In 1356, as we have noted earlier, Guilhelm Molinier drew on both the *De doctrina dicendi et tacendi* and the *Leys d'amors* for the last third of his work. The Ménagier de Paris also incorporated the abridged version of the *Liber consolationis* into his book of instructions for his young wife. From this point, the work was closely identified with northern culture.

When Geoffrey Chaucer adapted the *Liber consolationis* to become the "Tale of Melibee," its transformation was well advanced. The "Tale of Melibee" was no longer a tract against the urban vendetta; it had been transported not merely temporally but also ideologically into an environment dominated by great landed seigneurs.[19] Much the same kind of transformation also took place in Germany in the *Lere und Underweisung* and *Meister Albertus Lere,* fourteenth- and fifteenth-century adaptations which have been studied by J. Knight Bostock.[20] Albertanus's concerns with professional organization and means of resolving conflict were lost to more generalized appeals for peace and order. The development of law was not neglected, but no longer reflected the sophisticated structures of northern Italy. The relative neglect of Albertanus's other writings, particularly the *De amore,* meant that he was chiefly known as the author of a dramatic tale. It was as a moralist and as the author of the Tale of Melibeus that he would continue to exercise influence well into the sixteenth century.

Very little written in this chapter has been new, but it has been put in a new setting. Quite obviously, the concerns that motivated Albertanus of Brescia in the first half of the thirteenth century were only partially fulfilled in his evolving reputation. That is not to say that his theoretical work was entirely lost. We cannot know that. It very likely served some purpose in encouraging continued thinking about the relationship between the will of the individual and the norms set by the community. But a more relevant point for this volume is the role played by temporal and cultural factors in the shaping of Albertanus's influence on European thought. If intellectual history is to recognize the significance of figures like Albertanus, it must pay somewhat less attention to chains of ideas and more to the struggles of men like Albertanus to find a road to peace and order amid the turmoils of ordinary life.

Notes

1. John Knight Bostock, *Albertanus Brixiensis in Germany; Being an Account of Middle High German Translations from his Didactic Treatises* (London, 1924), 1–11; Saverio Panunzio, "Il codice Bargiacchi del volgarizzamento italiano del *Liber consolationis et consilii* di Albertano da Brescia," *Studi di filologia romanza offerti à Silvio Pellegrini* (Padua, 1971), 377–419, esp. 377–80.

2. Lodovico Muratori, *Opere*, in *Dal Muratori al Cesarotti*, ed. G. Falco and F. Forti (Milan, 1964) 1:1503–05.

3. Panunzio, "Il codice," 378.

4. Ibid., 378–79.

5. Brunetto Latini, *Li livres dou Tresor*, ed. Francis J. Carmody (Berkeley, Cal., 1948) 237–45.

6. Lauro Martines, "The Gentleman in Renaissance Italy: Strains of Isolation in the Body Politic," *The Darker Vision of the Renaissance* (Berkeley, Cal., 1974), 77–93.

7. Vatican City, BAV, Vat. Pal. Lat. 403 may well have been made for a clerical patron since it is in Latin. I am indebted to Kenneth Pennington for identifying it as Italian.

8. Nicola Zingarelli, "I trattati di Albertano da Brescia in dialetto veneziano," *Studi di letteratura italiana* 3 (1901): 151–92; Michele Barbi, "D'un antico codice pisano-lucchese di trattati morali," *Raccolta di studii critici dedicata ad Alessandro d'Ancona* (Florence, 1901), 241–59.

9. Aldo Checchini, "Un guidice del secolo decimoterzo: Albertano da Brescia," *Atti del reale istituto veneto di scienze, lettere, ed arti* 71:2 (1911–12): 1428; however, I have not been able to find any precise quotations from Albertanus in the *De volgare eloquentia*, nor any mention of his name by the poet. See note 10.

10. Santino Caramella, "Dante e Albertano da Brescia," *Studi letterari: Miscellanea in onore di Emilio Santini* (Palermo, 1956), 88–89. I am grateful for the suggestion made by a reader that there may be a connection in their views on towers. Cf. Maria Corti, "Dante e la torre di Babele: una nuova allegoria *in factis*," in *Il viaggio testuale: Le ideologie e le strutture semiotiche* (Turin, 1987), 243–56.

11. Maria Corti, "Le fonti del *Fiore di virtù* e la teoria della 'Nobilità' nel duecento," *Giornale storico della letteratura italiana* 71 (1959): 1–82.

12. Karl Vossler, *Medieval Culture: An Introduction to Dante and His Times*, 2 vols. (New York, 1966) 2:80.

13. Paris, Bibliothèque Nationale, Français, 19123. Henri was bishop of Metz.

14. Mario Roques, "Traductions françaises des traités moraux d'Albertano de Brescia," *Histoire literaire de la France* 37 (1936–38): 490–91. This valuable article provides the basis for the following discussion.

15. Ibid., 492–93.

16. Ibid., 497–99. This consisted in part of editing out references to the urban environment such as towers and to specific urban officials such as the *causidici* and the podestàs.

17. Ibid., 497–501.

18. Ibid., 502–3.

19. Gardner Stillwell, "The Political Meaning of Chaucer's *Tale of Melibee*," *Speculum* 19 (1944): 433–44; more recent discussion may be found in Paul Olson, *The Canterbury Tales and the Good Society* (Princeton, 1986), 113–23. The Spanish translation of the *Liber consolationis* provides interesting evidence of this process of transformation, too. Albertano da Brescia, *Llibre de consolacio i consell*, ed. G. E. Sansone (Barcelona, 1965), 95. Melibeus is referred to as "Cant Melibeu."

20. Bostock maintains that the *Meister Albertus Lere* was influenced by French models (*Albertanus Brixiensis*, 35). The transmission of *Lere und Underweisung* is less clear (22–27). Neither are faithful translations. *Meister Albertus Lere* is a free adaptation of the *De doctrina* and the *Liber consolationis* with a sermon text of Brother Peregrinus (34–42).

Appendix: A Note on the Manuscripts

THE LARGE NUMBER OF MANUSCRIPTS of the writings of Albertanus of Brescia presents a significant challenge to scholars, given the inadequacy of present editions. The following remarks represent the results of a preliminary survey of the manuscripts. Hopefully, they will be of some use to others working in the field.

There are three major groups of manuscripts, at least two of which may be further subdivided. Group A, which consists of manuscripts in which the treatises are arranged in order of their composition (*De amore, De doctrina dicendi et tacendi, Liber consolationis et consilii*), is found in such manuscripts as Pavia (Biblioteca Universitaria, 235 [thirteenth century]) and in several fourteenth- and fifteenth-century manuscripts.[1] It seems to be related to London (Lambeth, 375 [fourteenth century]), which also contains the sermons. Group B, which arranges the treatises in an order beginning with the *De doctrina dicendi et tacendi* and ending with the *De amore,* is much more common. Among its number is, most probably, Florence (Riccardiana 770 [thirteenth century]), which appears unique in the distinctive title it assigns to the *De amore.* A better example may be Madrid (Biblioteca Nacionál Lat. 411 [thirteenth century]), which is distinctive in having Lothar of Segni's (Innocent III) *De miseria* at the beginning of the manuscript.[2] A subgroup containing the sermons numbers such examples as Vatican City (BAV, Vat. Lat. 991 [thirteenth century]), Madrid (BN, Lat. 600 [thirteenth century]), Paris (Bibliothèque Nationale, Lat. 3345 [thirteenth/fourteenth century]), and Brescia (Queriniana, C VII 14 [fourteenth century; dated 1311]).[3] Group C places the *De amore* first and the *De doctrina* last, as in Milan (Ambrosiana B 40 Sup [thirteenth century]). There are also a considerable number of manuscripts in which only one or two treatises, usually the *De doctrina,* appear. Although logic suggests a priority for Group A, with the possibility that the subgroup containing the sermons is a somewhat later version, there is as yet no certainty that A is prior to B or even to C. More research remains to be done before a final decision can be reached.

Notes

1. Vienna, Bibliotheca Palatina, 322 (fifteenth century); Melk, Stiftsbibliothek, 45[B.9] (fourteenth century); Oxford, Magdelen College, Lat. 7 (fifteenth century).

2. These include: Vatican City, BAV, Vat. Lat. 992 (fourteenth century); London, Lambeth, 384 (fifteenth century); Paris, Bibliotheque Nationale, Lat. 3235 (fifteenth century); Paris, BN, Lat. 3347 (fifteenth century); Copenhagen, Royal Library, Lat. Thott 110 (fourteenth century), and Madrid, Biblioteca Nacionál, Lat. 1560 (fourteenth century).

3. See also Venice, Marciana, Lat. VI, 174 (3021) (Valentinelli, 35) (fourteenth century), which contains numerous other texts, including the *De miseria* of Innocent III. Another example is Vatican City, BAV, Vat. Pal. Lat. 403, a fifteenth-century manuscript done in a humanistic hand with illustrations.

Bibliography

MANUSCRIPTS

ALBERTANUS OF BRESCIA

I have not been able to consult all of these manuscripts. Those marked with an asterisk are not listed in Hiltz's dissertation.

Bresica. Queriniana, C VII 14 (fourteenth century; dated 1311). *De doctrina; Liber consolationis; De amore;* five sermons.

Cambridge. Corpus Christi College, 306 (fourteenth century, early). *De doctrina; Liber consolationis; De amore;* five sermons.

Cambridge. Gonville and Caius College, 61 (155) (fourteenth century). *De doctrina; Liber consolationis; De amore;* five sermons.

Cambridge. Sidney Sussex College, 48 Δ 3.3. (fifteenth century). *De doctrina; Liber consolationis; De amore;* five sermons.

Cambridge. University Library (1040) EE IV 23 (fourteenth century). *De doctrina; Liber consolationis; De amore;* five sermons.

*Copenhagen. Royal Library, Lat. Thott 110 (fourteenth century). *De doctrina; Liber consolationis; De amore.*

*Florence. Biblioteca Riccardiana, 770 (thirteenth century). *De doctrina; Liber consolationis; De amore.* Incomplete.

London. British Library, Add. 6158 (fourteenth century). *De doctrina; Liber consolationis; De amore;* sermons.

London. Lambeth, 375 (fourteenth century). *De amore; De doctrina; Liber consolationis;* five sermons.

London. Lambeth, 384 (fifteenth century). *De doctrina; Liber consolationis; De amore.*

Madrid. Biblioteca Nacionál, Lat. 411 (thirteenth century). *De amore; De doctrina; Liber consolationis.* Prefaced by Innocent III's *De miseria.*

Madrid. Biblioteca Nacionál, Lat. 600 (thirteenth century). *De doctrina; Liber consolationis; De amore;* five sermons.

Madrid. Biblioteca Nacionál, Lat. 1560 (fourteenth century). *De doctrina; Liber consolationis; De amore.*

Melk, Austria. Stiftsbibliothek, 45 (B.9.) (fourteenth century). *De amore; De doctrina; Liber consolationis.* Titles of treatises vary.

*Milan. Biblioteca Ambrosiana, B. 40 Sup. (thirteenth century). *De amore; Liber consolationis; De doctrina.*

*Milan. Biblioteca Ambrosiana, o 76 Sup. (thirteenth century). *De doctrina; Liber consolationis; De amore;* five sermons.

Oxford. Magdalen College, Lat. 7 (fifteenth century). *De amore; De doctrina; Liber consolationis.*

*Paris. Bibliothèque Nationale, Lat. 3235 (fifteenth century). *De doctrina; Liber consolationis; De amore.*

Paris. BN, Lat. 3345 (thirteenth/fourteenth century). *De doctrina; Liber consolationis; De amore;* five sermons.

*Paris. BN, Lat. 3346 (fourteenth century). *De doctrina; Liber consolationis; De amore;* five sermons.

*Paris. BN, Lat. 3347 (fifteenth century). *De doctrina; Liber consolationis; De amore.*

Paris. BN, Français, 19123 (fifteenth century). *Le Livre de Melibée et Prudence.*

Pavia. Biblioteca Universitaria, 235 (thirteenth century). *De amore; De doctrina; Liber consolationis.*

Vatican City. BAV, Vat. Lat. 401 (fourteenth century). *De doctrina; Liber consolationis; De amore;* five sermons. Titles of treatises vary.

*Vatican City. BAV, Vat. Lat. 991 (thirteenth century). *De doctrina; Liber consolationis; De amore;* five sermons.

*Vatican City. BAV, Vat. Lat. 992 (fourteenth century). *De doctrina; Liber consolationis; De amore.*

*Vatican City. BAV, Vat. Lat. 993 (fourteenth century). *De doctrina; Liber consolationis; De amore;* five sermons.

*Vatican City. BAV, Vat. Lat. 2746 (fourteenth century). *De doctrina; Liber consolationis; De amore;* five sermons.

*Vatican City. BAV, Vat. Lat. 5996 (fourteenth century). *De doctrina; Liber consolationis; De amore;* five sermons.

*Vatican City. BAV, Vat. Pal. Lat. 403 (fifteenth century). *De doctrina; Liber consolationis; De amore.* Humanistic script. Illustrated.

Venice. Biblioteca Marciana, Lat. VI, 174 (3021) Valentinelli, 35 (fourteenth century). *De doctrina; Liber consolationis; De amore;* five sermons. Contains other materials, including extracts from Seneca and Innocent III's *De miseria.*

Vienna. Bibliotheca Palatina, 322 (fifteenth century). *De amore; De doctrina; Liber consolationis.*

ST. AUGUSTINE

Brescia. Queriniana, G III 3 (tenth century). *De civitate Dei.*

SENECA

Brescia. Queriniana, B II 6 (tenth century). *Epistolae morales ad Lucilium.*

DOCUMENT

Milan. Archivio di Stato. Fondi religiosi. SS. Cosmo e Damiano. Cart. 65 (13 August 1249).

PRINTED SOURCES

PRIMARY SOURCES (MODERN EDITIONS) FOR ALBERTANUS OF BRESCIA

"*De amore et dilectione Dei et proximi et aliarum rerum et de forma vitae:* An Edition." Edited by Sharon Hiltz. Ph.D. diss., University of Pennsylvania, 1980.
De arte loquendi et tacendi. In Thor Sundby, *Della vita e delle opere di Brunetto Latini*, 475–509. Florence, 1884.
Dei trattati morali di Albertano da Brescia. Edited by Francesco Selmi. Bologna, 1873.
Liber consolationis et consilii. Edited by Thor Sundby. Copenhagen, 1873.
Llibre de consolacio i consell. Edited by G. E. Sansone. Barcelona, 1965.
Sermone inedito di Albertano, giudice di Brescia. Edited by Luigi F. Fè d'Ostiani. Brescia, 1874.
Sermones quattuor: Edizione curate sui codici bresciani. Edited by Marta Ferrari. Lonato, 1955.
Soffredi del Grathia's Uebersetzung der philosophischen Traktate Albertano's von Brescia. Edited by Gustav Rolin. Leipzig, 1898.

OTHER PRIMARY SOURCES

Alcuin. *De Rhetorica: The Rhetoric of Alcuin and Charlemagne.* Princeton, 1941.
André le Chapelain. *Traité de l'amour courtois.* Translated by Claude Buridant. Paris, 1974.
Annales brixienses. MGHSS, Vol. 18.
Annales parmenses maiores. MGHSS, Vol. 18.
Annales placentini guelphi. MGHSS, Vol. 18.
Augustinus Aurelius. *De civitate Dei.* 2 vols. Corpus Christianorum, vols. 47–48. Tournai, 1955.
———. "Regula." *PL* 32:1377–84.
Boethius. *The Consolation of Philosophy.* Cambridge, Mass., 1946.
Boncompagno da Signa. *Amicitia.* Edited by Sarina Nathan. Rome, 1909.
———. *Rhetorica novissima*, 2:251–97. Bibliotheca Iuridica Medii Aevi. Edited by A. Gaudenzi. Bologna, 1901.
The Book of the Thousand Nights and One Night. 4 vols. London, 1972.
Caecilius Balbus. *Sententiae.* Edited by Edward Woefflin. Basle, 1855.
Caesarius of Heisterbach. *The Dialogue of Miracles.* 2 vols. London, 1929.

Cicero, Marcus Tullius. *De inventione*. Cambridge, Mass., 1968.

Codice diplomatico del senato romano dal MCXLIV al MCCCXLVII. Edited by Franco Bartaloni. Fonti per la storia d'Italia, vol. 87. Rome, 1948.

Conciliorum oecumenicorum decreta. Bologna, 1973.

Corpus juris canonici. Edited by Emil Friedberg. 2 vols. Graz, 1959.

Dante Alighieri. *Opere*. Edited by E. Moore and Paget Toynbee. 4th ed. Oxford, 1963.

The Florentine Fior di virtù of 1491. Translated by Nicholas Fersin. Washington, D.C., 1953.

Godofredus Prior. *Epigrammata*. *RS* 59:2.

Guerrini, Paolo. "Gli statuti di un'antica congregazione francescana di Brescia." *Archivum franciscanum historicum*. 1 (1908): 544–47.

Hugh of St. Victor. *Didascalicon: A Medieval Guide to the Arts*. Edited and translated by Jerome Taylor. New York, 1961.

Huillard-Bréholles, Jean L. A. *Historia diplomatica Friderici Secundi*. 6 vols. Paris, 1852–61.

Innocent III. *De miseria condicionis humanae*. Athens, Ga., 1978.

Jacobus de Vitriaco. *Historia occidentalis*. Edited by John F. Hinnebusch. Freiburg, 1972.

Joannes de Viterbo. *Liber de regimine civitatum*. Edited by G. Salvemini. *Bibliotheca Iuridica Medii Aevi*, edited by A. Gaudenzi, vol. 3. Bologna, 1901.

Die Konstitutionen Friedrich II für sein Königreich Sizilien. Cologne, 1973.

Latini, Brunetto. *Li Livres dou tresor*. Edited by Francis J. Carmody, Berkeley, Cal., 1948.

Liber potheris communis civitatis Brixiae. *Historiae Patriae Monumenta*, vol. 19. Turin, 1899.

Martin, Archibishop of Braga. *Opera*. Edited by Claude Barlow. New Haven, 1950.

Matthew Paris. Ex Mattaei Parisiensis *Cronicis Maioribus*. *MGHSS*, 28.

Meersseman, Gérard G. *Dossier de l'ordre de pénitence*. Paris, 1982.

———. "Il manuale dei penitenti di Brescia," 1:410–34. *Ordo fraternitatis: Confraternite e pietà dei laici nel medioevo*. 3 vols. Rome, 1977.

Le ménagier de Paris. 2 vols. Paris, 1816.

Monumenta Germaniae Historica. *Epistolae Saeculi XIII*. 3 vols. Edited by Carl Rodenberg. Munich, 1982. Vol. 1 only.

Das moralium philosophorum de Guillaume de Conches. Edited by John Holmberg. Uppsala, 1929.

Muratori, Lodovico. *Antiquitates Italicae medii aevi*. 6 vols. Milan, 1738–42.

———. *Opere*. In *Dal Muratori al Cesarotti*. Edited by G. Falco and F. Forti. 2 vols. Milan, 1964.

———. *Rerum Italicarum scriptores*. 28 vols. Milan, 1723–51.

Oculus Pastoralis. In Lodovico Muratori. *Antiquitates Italicae medii aevi*, 4:95–128. Milan, 1738–42.

Ovidius Naso, Publius. *Remedia amoris*. Cambridge, Mass., 1969.

Pamphilus de Amore. *Three Latin Comedies*. Toronto, 1976.

Le Pergamene del monastero di S. Giulia di Brescia, 1043–1590. *Monumenta Brixiensis Historica*, vol. 7. Edited by Rosa Zilioli Faden. Brescia, 1984.

Le Pergamene degli Umiliati di Cremona. Edited by Vincenzo d'Alessandro. Palermo, 1964.

Peter of Blois. *De amicitia et de caritate Dei et proximi. PL* 207:871–958.

Petrus Alfonsi. *The Disciplina clericalis of Petrus Alfonsi.* Berkeley, Cal., 1977.

Publilius Syrus. *Sententiae.* Leipzig, 1880.

Raimund de Biterris. *Liber kalilae et dimnae.* In *Les fabulistes Latins depuis le siècle d'Auguste jusqu'à la fin du moyen âge.* Edited by Léopold Hervieux. 5 vols. 1893–90. Reprint. Hildesheim, 1970. Vol. 5.

Regesta Honorii Papae III. Edited by Petrus Pressutti. 2 vols. 1888. Reprint. Hildesheim, 1978.

Rhetores Latini minores. Edited by Carolus Halm. Leipzig, 1863.

Rockinger, Ludwig, ed. *Briefsteller und Formelbücher des elften bis vierzehnten Jahrhunderts.* Quellen und Erörterungen zur bayerischen und deutschen Geschichte, vol. 9. Munich, 1963.

Rolandinus Patavinus. *Cronica marchiae trivixane. RISS* n.s., vol. 8.

Seneca, Lucius Annaeus. *Ad Lucilium epistulae morales.* 3 vols. (Loeb ed.) Cambridge, Mass., 1930–34.

Statuti di confraternite religiose di Padova nel medioevo. Edited by Giuseppina de Sandre Gasparini. Fonti e ricerche di storia ecclesiastica padovana, vol. 6. Padua, 1974.

Thierry of Chartres. *The Latin Rhetorical Commentaries.* Edited by Karen Fredborg. Toronto, 1988.

Ughelli, Ferdinando. *Italia Sacra.* 2d ed. 9 vols. Venice, 1717–22. Reprint, Nendeln, Liecht., 1970.

Virgilius Maro, Publius. *The Georgics and Eclogues of Vergil.* Cambridge, Mass., 1915.

Wakefield, Walter, and Austin P. Evans. *Heresies of the High Middle Ages: Selected Sources Translated and Annotated.* New York, 1969.

Walter of Chatillon. *Moralisch-satirische Gedichte.* Edited by Karl Strecker. Heidelberg, 1929.

SECONDARY SOURCES

Abeni, Enzo. *La storia bresciana: Il frammento e l'insieme.* 4 vols. Brescia, 1987.

Baker, Herschel C. *The Dignity of Man: Studies in the Persistence of an Idea.* Cambridge, Mass., 1947.

Baldwin, John W. *Masters, Princes, and Merchants: The Social Views of Peter the Chanter and his Circle.* 2 vols. Princeton, 1970.

Balestrini, Fausto. *Uomini di Brescia.* Brescia, 1987.

Banker, James R. *Death in the Community: Memorialization and Confraternities in an Italian Commune in the Late Middle Ages.* Athens, Ga., 1988.

Barbi, Michele. "D'un antico codice pisano-lucchese di trattati morali." *Raccolta di studii critici dedicata ad Alessandro d'Ancona,* 241–59. Florence, 1901.

Baron, Hans. "Cicero and the Roman Civic Spirit." *Bulletin of the John Rylands Library* 22 (1938): 72–83.

————. "Franciscan Poverty and Civic Wealth as Factors in the Rise of Humanistic Thought." *Speculum* 13 (1938): 1–37.

————. *In Search of Florentine Civic Humanism: Essays on the Transition from the Medieval to Modern Thought.* 2 vols. Princeton, 1988.

Baronio, Angelo. *Monasterium et populus: Per la storia del contado lombardo, Leno.* Brescia, 1984.

Becker, G. *Catalogi bibliothecarum antiqui.* Bonn, 1885.

Becker, Marvin. *Civility and Society in Western Europe, 1300–1600.* Bloomington, Ind., 1988.

Beloch, Karl Julius. *Berölkerungsgeschichte Italiens.* 3 vols. Berlin, 1937–61.

Benson, Robert L. "Protohumanism and Narrative Technique in Early Thirteenth-Century Italian 'Ars Dictaminis.'" *Boccaccio: Secoli di vita: Atti del congresso internazionale: Boccaccio, 1975.* Edited by Marga Cottino-Jones and Edward Tuttle, 31–50. Ravenna, 1977.

Billanovich, Giuseppe. *I primi umanisti e le tradizione dei classici italiani.* Freiburg, Switz., 1953.

Biller, Peter. "Medieval Waldensian Abhorrence of Killing, pre-ca. 1400." *Studies in Church History* 20 (1983): 129–46.

Black, Christopher. *Italian Confraternities in the Sixteenth Century.* Cambridge, 1989.

Bloomfield, Morton. *The Incipits of Latin Works on the Virtues and Vices, 1100–1500 A.D.* Cambridge, Mass., 1979.

Borst, Arno. *Die Katharer.* Schriften der Monumenta Germaniae Historica, vol. 12. Stuttgart, 1953.

Bosisio, Alfredo. "Brescia ai tempi di Federico II (1220–1250)." *Storia di Brescia* 1:655–76.

Bostock, John Knight. *Albertanus Brixiensis in Germany; Being an Account of Middle High German Translations from his Didactic Treatises.* London, 1924.

Brontesi, Alfredo. "Guala, vescovo di Brescia." *Bibliotheca Sanctorum* 7:412–19. Rome, 1961–70.

Brundage, James A. "The Medieval Advocate's Profession." *Law and History Review* 6 (1988): 439–64.

Burckhardt, Jacob. *Die Kultur der Renaissance in Italien.* 13th ed. Leipzig, 1922.

Bynum, Carolyn Walker. *Holy Feast and Holy Fast.* Berkeley, Cal., 1987.

Caramella, Santino. "Dante e Albertano da Brescia." *Studi letterari: Miscellanea in onore di Emilio Santini,* 87–94. Palermo, 1956.

Cavriolo, Elia. *Dell'istorie della città di Brescia.* Venice, 1744.

Checchini, Aldo. "Un giudice del secolo decimoterzo: Albertano da Brescia." *Atti del reale istituto veneto di scienze, lettere, ed arti* 71:2 (1911–12): 1423–95.

Chiffoleau, Jacques. "Entre le religieux et le politique: Les confréries du Saint-Esprit en Provence et en comtat Venaissin à la fin du moyen âge." In *Le mouvement confraternel au moyel âge,* 9–40. Geneva, 1987.

Constable, Giles. "The Diversity of Religious Life and the Acceptance of Social Pluralism in the Twelfth Century." In *History, Society and the Churches: Essays in Honour of Owen Chadwick,* edited by Derek Beales and Geoffrey Best, 29–47. Cambridge, 1985.

Corti, Maria. "Dante e la torre di Babele: Una nuova allegoria *in factis*." In *Il viaggio testuale: Le ideologie e le strutture semiotiche*, 243–56. Turin, 1987.

———. "Le fonti del *Fiore di virtù* e le teoria della 'Nobiltà' nel duecento." *Giornale storico della letteratura italiana* 71 (1959): 1–82.

Cussutta, Fabio. *Gli umanisti e la rhetorica*. Rome, 1984.

Coulet, Noel. "Le mouvement confraternel en Provence et dans le comtat Venaissin au moyen âge." In *Le mouvement confraternel au moyen âge*, 83–110. Geneva, 1987.

Cracco, Giorgio. "Da Commune di famiglie à città satellite." *Storia di Vicenza* 2:99–110. Vicenza, 1988.

———. *Storia di Vicenza*. 2 vols. Vicenza, 1987–88.

Davis, Charles T. *Dante's Italy and Other Essays*. Philadelphia, 1984.

Davy M., *Un traité de l'amour du XII^c siècle–Pierre de Blois*. Paris, 1932.

Dondaine, Antoine. "La hierarchie cathare en Italie." *Archivum fratrum praedicatorum* 20 (1950): 234–324.

Evans, Gillian R. *Old Arts and New Theology*. Oxford, 1980.

Faden, Rosa Zilioli. *Catalogo inventoriale dei manoscritti della raccolta Odorici*. Brescia, 1988.

Falsina, Luigi. *Santi e chiese della diocesi di Brescia*. Brescia, 1969.

Fè d'Ostiani, Luigi F. "I conti rurali bresciani del medioevo." *Archivio storico lombardo* 26 (1899): 5–55.

Ferrari, Marta. "Intorno ad alcuni sermoni inediti di Albertano da Brescia." *Atti del istituto veneto di scienze, lettere ed arti* 109 (1950–51): 69–93.

Ferreiro, Albert. "St. Martin of Braga's Policy toward Heretics and Pagan Practices." *American Benedictine Review* 34:4 (1983): 372–95.

Finoli, Anna Maria. "La cultura à Brescia nel medioevo." *Storia di Brescia* 1:971–97.

Fonseca, Cosimo D. *Medioevo canonicale*. Milan, 1970.

Frugoni, A. *Arnoldo da Brescia nelle fonti del secolo XII*. Rome, 1954.

Garver, Eugene *Machiavelli and the History of Prudence*. Madison, Wis., 1987.

Greenaway, George W. *Arnold of Brescia*. New York, 1978.

Gregorovius, Ferdinand. *History of the City of Rome in the Middle Ages*. 6 vols. London, 1903–12.

Guerrini, Paolo. *Una celebre famiglia lombarda. I conti di Martinengo*. Brescia, 1930.

Heers, Jacques. *Parties and Political Life in the Medieval West*. New York, 1977.

Hiltz, Sharon. "*De amore et dilectione Dei et proximi et aliarum rerum et de forma vitae:* An Edition." Ph.D. diss., University of Pennsylvania, 1980.

Historiographie du catharisme. Toulouse, 1979.

Hyde, John K. "Contemporary Views on Faction and Civil Strife in Thirteenth- and Fourteenth-Century Italy." In *Violence and Civil Disorder*, edited by Lauro Martines, 273–307. Berkeley, Cal., 1972.

———. *Padua in the Age of Dante*. Manchester, 1966.

———. *Society and Politics in Medieval Italy: The Evolution of Civil Life*. London, 1973.

Kantorowicz, Ernst H. *The King's Two Bodies: A Study of Medieval Political Theology*. Princeton, 1957.

Kristeller, Paul. *Iter Italicum.* 3 vols. to date. London, 1963–83.

Lambert, Malcolm. *Medieval Heresy.* London, 1977.

Lapidge, Michael. "The Stoic Inheritance." *A History of Twelfth-Century Philosophy,* 81–121. Cambridge, 1988.

Laurenti, Milva. "Violenza, guerra, pena di morte: le proposte degli eretici medievali." *Rivista di Storia delle chiesa in Italia* 43 (1989): 123–31.

Lawrence, C. H. *Medieval Monasticism.* 2d ed. London, 1984.

Letteratura italiana. Il letterato e le istituzioni. Edited by A. A. Rosa. Turin, 1982. Vol. 1 only.

Little, Lester. *Liberty, Charity, Fraternity: Lay Religious Confraternities in Bergamo in the Age of the Commune.* Bergamo, 1988.

———. *Religious Poverty and the Profit Economy in Medieval Europe.* Ithaca, N.Y., 1978.

Lucas, Angela M. *Women in the Middle Ages.* New York, 1983.

McDonnell, Ernest W. "The Vita Apostolica: Diversity or Dissent." *Church History* 24 (1955): 15–31.

Mainzer, Conrad. "Albertano of Brescia's *Liber Consolationis et Consilii* as a Sourcebook of Gower's *Confessio Amantis.*" *Medium Aevum* 47 (1978): 88–89.

Malvezzi, Jacopo. *Chronicon Brixianum. RISS,* 14.

Manselli, Raoul. *L'eresia del male.* Naples, 1961.

Mariella, Antonino. *Le origini degli ospedali bresciani.* Brescia, 1963.

Martines, Lauro. "The Gentleman in Renaissance Italy: Strains of Isolation in the Body Politic." *The Darker Vision of the Renaissance,* 77–93. Berkeley, Cal., 1974.

———. "Political Violence in the Thirteenth Century." In *Violence and Civil Disorder,* edited by Lauro Martinez, 331–53. Berkeley, Cal., 1972.

———. *Power and Imagination: City-States in Renaissance Italy.* New York, 1979.

———. *Violence and Disorder in Italian Cities, 1200–1500.* Berkeley, Cal., 1972.

Mazzatinti, G. "La lezenda di Fra Rainiero Faxano." *Bolletino della società umbra di storia patria* 2 (1896): 561–65.

Meersseman, Gérard G. *Ordo Fraternitatis: Confraternite e pietà dei laici nel medioevo.* 3 vols. Rome, 1977.

———. "Pénitents ruraux communautaires en Italie au XIIᶜ siècle." *Revue d'histoire ecclésiastique* 49 (1954): 343–90.

———. "Per la storiografia delle confraternite nel medioevo." *Ordo Fraternitatis* 1: 3–34.

———. "Predicatori laici nelle confraternite medievali," *Ordo Fraternitatis* 3: 1273–89.

———. "Seneca maestro di spiritualità nei suoi opusculi apocrifi dal XII al XV secolo." *Italia medioevale e umanistica* 16 (1973): 43–133.

Meredith, Jill. "The Revival of the Augustan Age in the Court Art of Frederick II." In *Artistic Strategy and the Rhetoric of Power,* edited by David Castriota, 39–56. Carbondale, Ill. 1986.

Mollat, Michel. *The Poor in the Middle Ages.* New Haven, 1986.

Monti, Gennaro M. *Le confraternite medievali dell'alta e media Italia.* 2 vols. Venice, 1927.

Moorman, John R. H. *A History of the Franciscan Order from its Origins to the Year 1517.* Oxford, 1968.

Morghen, Raffaello. *Medioevo cristiano.* Bari, 1951.

Morrison, Karl. *The Mimetic Tradition of Reform in the West.* Princeton, 1982.

Le Mouvement confraternel au moyen âge: France, Italie, Suisse. Actes de la table ronde organisée par l'université de Lausanne. Geneva, 1987.

Murphy, James J. *Rhetoric in the Middle Ages: A History of Rhetorical Theory from St. Augustine to the Renaissance.* Berkeley, Cal., 1974

———. *Medieval Rhetoric: A Select Bibliography.* Toronto, 1989.

Murray, Alexander. "Piety and Impiety in Thirteenth-Century Italy." *Studies in Church History* 8 (1972): 83–106.

Nothdurft, Klaus-Dieter. *Studien zum Einfluss Senecas auf die Philosophie und Theologie des zwölften Jahrhunderts.* Leiden-Cologne, 1963.

Odorici, Federico. *Storie bresciane dai primi tempi sino all'età nostra.* 11 vols. Brescia, 1853–65.

Olson, Paul. *The Canterbury Tales and the Good Society.* Princeton, 1986.

Osheim, Duane. *An Italian Lordship: The Bishopric of Lucca in the Late Middle Ages.* Berkeley, Cal., 1977.

Owen, Charles. "The Tale of Melibee." *The Chaucer Review* 7 (1973): 267–80.

Panunzio, Saverio. "Il codice Bargiacchi del volgarizzamento italiano del *Liber consolationis et consilii* di Albertano da Brescia." *Studi di filologia romanza offerti à Silvio Pellegrini,* 377–419. Padua, 1971.

Peemens-Poullet, Hedwige. *Principes, Pédagogues, et classes sociales au XIII^c siècle.* 2 vols. Thése de 3eme cycle. Paris X–Nanterre, 1975.

Penco, Gregorio. *Storia della chiesa in Italia.* 2 vols. Milan, 1977.

Peters, Edward. "The Frowning Pages: Scythians, Garamites, Florentines, and the Two Laws." In *The Divine Comedy and the Encyclopedia of the Arts and Sciences,* edited by Giuseppe C. Di Scipio and Aldo Scaglione, 285–314. Amsterdam, 1988.

———. "Pars, parte: Dante and an Urban Contribution to Political Thought." In *The Medieval City,* edited by Harry Miskimin, 113–40. New Haven, 1977.

Pocock, J. G. A. *The Machiavellian Moment: Florentine Political Thought and the Atlantic Republican Tradition.* Princeton, 1975.

———. *Politics, Language, and Time.* New York, 1971.

Post, Gaines. "A Romano-Canonical Maxim, *Quod omnes tangit,* in Bracton and Early Parliaments." In *Studies in Medieval Legal Thought,* 163–238. Princeton, 1964.

Powell, James M. *Anatomy of a Crusade, 1213–1221.* Philadelphia, 1986.

———. "Economy and Society in the Kingdom of Sicily under Frederick II." Washington, D.C., forthcoming.

———. "The Papacy and the Early Franciscans." *Franciscan Studies.* 36 (1976): 248–62.

Renaissance Humanism: Foundations, Forms and Legacies. Edited by Albert Rabil. 3 vols. Philadelphia, 1988.

Reynolds, Leighton D. *The Medieval Tradition of Seneca's Letters.* London, 1965.

The Rich, the Well-Born, and the Powerful: Elites and Upper Classes in History. Edited by Frederic C. Jaher. Urbana, Ill., 1973.

Rigon, Antonio. "Chiesa e vita religiosa à Padova nel duecento." *S. Antonio: 1231–1981: Il suo tempo, il suo culto, e la sua città,* 284–307. Padua, 1981.

———. "Le congregazioni del clero urbano in area veneta (XII–XV Sec.)." In *Le mouvement confraternel au moyen âge,* 343–60. Geneva, 1987.

Roques, Mario. "Traductions françaises des traités moraux d'Albertano de Brescia." *Histoire literaire de la France* 37 (1936–38): 488–506.

Rubenstein, Nicolai. "Some Ideas on Municipal Progress and Decline in the Italy of the Communes." In *Fritz Saxl Memorial Essays,* 165–83. London, 1957.

Ruggiero, Guido. *Violence in Early Renaissance Venice.* New Brunswick, N.J., 1980.

Salvemini, Gaetano. "Il 'Liber de regimine civitatum.'" *Giornale storico della literatura italiano* 41 (1903): 283–303.

Savini, Savino. *Il catarismo italiano ed i suoi vescovi nei secoli XIII e XIV.* Florence, 1958.

Seigel, Jerrold. *Rhetoric and Philosophy in Renaissance Humanism: The Union of Eloquence and Wisdom, Petrarch to Valla.* Princeton, 1968.

Skinner, Quentin. *The Foundations of Modern Political Thought.* 2 vols. Cambridge, 1978.

———. "Political Philosophy." In *The Cambridge History of Renaissance Philosophy,* edited by Charles Schmitt, 389–452. Cambridge, 1988.

Smalley, Beryl. *English Friars and Antiquity in the Early Fourteenth Century.* Oxford, 1960.

Stillwell, Gardner. "The Political Meaning of Chaucer's 'Tale of Melibee.'" *Speculum* 19 (1944): 433–44.

La storia di Brescia. Edited by Giovanni Treccani degli Alfieri. 4 vols. Brescia, 1963.

Storia d'Italia. Edited by G. Galasso. Turin, 1981. Vol. 4 only.

Sundby, Thor. *Della vita e delle opere di Brunetto Latini.* Florence, 1884.

Tierney, Brian. *Religion, Law, and the Growth of Constitutional Thought, 1150–1650.* Cambridge, 1983.

Trebeschi, Cesare. "Albertano da Brescia." In *Uomini di Brescia,* edited by Fausto Balestrini, 93–109. Brescia, 1987.

Trexler, Richard C. "Charity and the Defence of Urban Elites in the Italian Communes." In *The Rich, the Well-Born, and the Powerful,* edited by Frederic C. Jaher, 64–109. Urbana, Ill. 1973.

Vaglia, Ugo, *Memorie illustri bresciani.* Brescia, 1958.

———. "I mercati della Valle Sabbia." *Archivio storico lombardo,* ser. 8, vol. 10 (1960): 116–30.

———. *Storia della Valle Sabbia.* 2 vols. Brescia, 1954.

Valentini, Andrea. *Il liber potheris della città e del comune di Brescia e la serie dei suoi consoli e podestà dall'anno 969 al 1438.* Brescia, 1878.

Vauchez, Andre. *Les laïcs au moyen âge.* Paris, 1987.

———. *La spiritualité de moyen âge occidental; VIIIᵉ–XIIᵉ siècles.* Paris, 1975.

Verbeke, Gerard. *The Presence of Stoicism in Medieval Thought*. Washington, D.C., 1983.

Verdon, J. "Le fonti per una storia della donna in Occidente." In *Donna nel medioevo: Aspetti culturali e di vita quotidiana,* edited by Maria de Matteis, 175–223. Bologna, 1986.

Verheijen, Luc de. *La règle de Saint Augustin*. 2 vols. Paris, 1967.

Villa, Claudia. "La tradizione delle 'Ad Lucilium' e la cultura di Brescia dall' età carolingia ad Albertano." *Italia medioevale e umanistica* 12 (1969): 9–51.

Violante, Cinzio. "La chiesa bresciana dall'inizio del secolo XIII al dominio veneto." *Storia di Brescia* 1: 1064–1124.

———. *La pataria milanese e la riforma ecclesiastica*. Roman, 1955.

———. *Studi sulla cristianità medioevale*. 2d ed. Milan, 1975.

Volpe, Gioacchino. *Movimenti religiosi e sette ereticali nella società medievale italiana*. Florence, 1922.

Vossler, Karl. *Medieval Culture: An Introduction to Dante and his Times*. 2 vols. New York, 1966.

Wakefield, Walter. *Heresy, Crusade, and Inquisition in Southern France, 1100–1250*. London, 1974.

Waley, Daniel. *The Italian City-Republics*. 3d ed. London, 1988.

Walker, David M. *The Oxford Companion to Law*. Oxford, 1980.

Weiss, Roberto. *Il primo secolo del umanesimo*. Rome, 1949.

Wickham, Chris J. *The Mountains and the City: The Tuscan Appenines in the Early Middle Ages*. Oxford, 1988.

Wieruszowski, Helene. "Rhetoric and the Classics in Italian Education of the Thirteenth Century." *Politics and Culture in Medieval Spain and Italy,* 589–627. Rome, 1971.

Zanella, Gabriele. *Machiavella prima di Machiavelli*. Bologna, 1985.

Zanoni, L. *Gli umiliati nei loro rapporti con l'eresia, l'industria della lana e i comuni nel secolo XII e XIII*. Milan, 1911.

Zingarelli, Nicola. "I trattati di Albertano da Brescia in dialetto veneziano." *Studi di letteratura italiana* 3 (1901): 151–92.

Index

University of Pennsylvania Press
MIDDLE AGES SERIES
Edward Peters, General Editor

Books in the series that are out of print are marked with an asterisk.

F. R. P. Akehurst, trans. *The* Coutumes de Beauvaisis *of Philippe de Beaumanoir.*
1992

David Anderson. *Before the Knight's Tale: Imitation of Classical Epic in Boccaccio's* Teseida. 1988

Benjamin Arnold. *Count and Bishop in Medieval Germany: A Study of Regional Power, 1100–1350.* 1992

J. M. W. Bean. *From Lord to Patron: Lordship in Late Medieval England.* 1990

Uta-Renate Blumenthal. *The Investiture Controversy: Church and Monarchy from the Ninth to the Twelfth Century.* 1988

Daniel Bornstein, trans. *Dino Compagni's Chronicle of Florence.* 1986.

Betsy Bowden. *Chaucer Aloud: The Varieties of Textual Interpretation.* 1987

James William Brodman. *Ransoming Captives in Crusader Spain: The Order of Merced on the Christian-Islamic Frontier.* 1986

Otto Brunner (Howard Kaminsky and James Van Horn Melton, eds. and trans.). Land *and Lordship: Structures of Governance in Medieval Austria.* 1991

Robert I. Burns, S.J., ed. *Emperor of Culture: Alfonso X the Learned of Castile and His Thirteenth-Century Renaissance.* 1990

David Burr. *Olivi and Franciscan Poverty: The Origins of the* Usus Pauper *Controversy.* 1989

Thomas Cable. *The English Alliterative Tradition.* 1991

Leonard Cantor, ed. *The English Medieval Landscape.* 1982*

Anthony K. Cassell and Victoria Kirkham, eds. and trans. *Diana's Hunt. Caccia di Diana. Boccaccio's First Fiction.* 1991

Brigitte Cazelles. *The Lady as Saint: A Collection of French Hagiographic Romances of the Thirteenth Century.* 1991

Willene B. Clark and Meradith T. McMunn, eds. *Beasts and Birds of the Middle Ages: The Bestiary and Its Legacy.* 1989

G. G. Coulton. *From St. Francis to Dante: Translations from the Chronicle of the Franciscan Salimbene (1221–1288).* 1972*

Richard C. Dales. *The Scientific Achievement of the Middle Ages.* 1973

Charles T. Davis. *Dante's Italy and Other Essays.* 1984

George T. Dennis, trans. *Maurice's Strategikon: Handbook of Byzantine Military Strategy.* 1984*

Katherine Fischer Drew, trans. *The Burgundian Code: The Book of Constitutions or Law of Gundobad and Additional Enactments.* 1972

Katherine Fischer Drew, trans. *The Laws of the Salian Franks.* 1991

Katherine Fischer Drew, trans. *The Lombard Laws.* 1973

Nancy Edwards. *The Archaeology of Early Medieval Ireland.* 1990

Margaret J. Ehrhart. *The Judgment of the Trojan Prince Paris in Medieval Literature.* 1987

Patrick J. Geary. *Aristocracy in Provence: The Rhône Basin at the Dawn of the Carolingian Age.* 1985

Julius Goebel, Jr. *Felony and Misdemeanor: A Study in the History of Criminal Law.* 1976*

Avril Henry, ed. *The Mirour of Mans Saluacioune: A Middle English Translation of* Speculum Humanae Salvationis. 1987

J. N. Hillgarth, ed. *Christianity and Paganism, 350–750: The Conversion of Western Europe.* 1986

Richard C. Hoffmann. *Land, Liberties, and Lordship in a Late Medieval Countryside: Agrarian Structures and Change in the Duchy of Wrocław.* 1990

Robert Hollander. *Boccaccio's Last Fiction: "Il Corbaccio."* 1988

Edward B. Irving, Jr. *Rereading* Beowulf. 1989

C. Stephen Jaeger. *The Origins of Courtliness: Civilizing Trends and the Formation of Courtly Ideals, 939–1210.* 1985

William Chester Jordan. *The French Monarchy and the Jews: From Philip Augustus to the Last Capetians.* 1989

William Chester Jordan. *From Servitude to Freedom: Manumission in the Sénonais in the Thirteenth Century.* 1986

Ellen E. Kittell. *From* Ad Hoc *to Routine: A Case Study in Medieval Bureaucracy.* 1991

Alan C. Kors and Edward Peters, eds. *Witchcraft in Europe, 1100–1700: A Documentary History.* 1972

Barbara M. Kreutz. *Before the Normans: Southern Italy in the Ninth and Tenth Centuries.* 1991

Jeanne Krochalis and Edward Peters, ed. and trans. *The World of Piers Plowman.* 1975

E. Ann Matter. *The Voice of My Beloved: The Song of Songs in Western Medieval Christianity.* 1990

María Rosa Menocal. *The Arabic Role in Medieval Literary History.* 1987

A. J. Minnis. *Medieval Theory of Authorship.* 1988

Lawrence Nees. *A Tainted Mantle: Hercules and the Classical Tradition at the Carolingian Court.* 1991

Lynn H. Nelson, trans. *The Chronicle of San Juan de la Peña: A Fourteenth-Century Offical History of the Crown of Aragon.* 1991

Charlotte A. Newman. *The Anglo-Norman Nobility in the Reign of Henry I: The Second Generation.* 1988

Thomas F. X. Noble. *The Republic of St. Peter: The Birth of the Papal State, 680–825.* 1984

Joseph F. O'Callaghan. *The Cortes of Castile-León, 1188–1350.* 1989

William D. Paden, ed. *The Voice of the Trobairitz: Perspectives on the Women Troubadours.* 1989

Kenneth Pennington. *Pope and Bishops: The Papal Monarchy in the Twelfth and Thirteenth Centuries.* 1984*

Edward Peters. *The Magician, the Witch, and the Law.* 1982

Edward Peters, ed. *Christian Society and the Crusades, 1198–1229.* Sources in Translation, including The Capture of Damietta by Oliver of Paderborn. 1971

Edward Peters, ed. *The First Crusade: The Chronicle of Fulcher of Chartres and Other Source Materials.* 1971

Edward Peters, ed. *Heresy and Authority in Medieval Europe.* 1980

Edward Peters, ed. *Monks, Bishops, and Pagans: Christian Culture in Gaul and Italy, 500–700.* 1975*

Clifford Peterson. *Saint Erkenwald.* 1977*

James M. Powell. *Albertanus of Brescia.* 1992.

James M. Powell. *Anatomy of a Crusade, 1213–1221.* 1986

Donald E. Queller. *The Fourth Crusade: The Conquest of Constantinople, 1201–1204.* 1977*

Michael Resler, trans. *EREC by Hartmann von Aue.* 1987

Pierre Riché (Jo Ann McNamara, trans.). *Daily Life in the World of Charlemagne.* 1978

Jonathan Riley-Smith. *The First Crusade and the Idea of Crusading.* 1986

Joel T. Rosenthal. *Patriarchy and Families of Privilege in Fifteenth-Century England.* 1991

Barbara H. Rosenwein. *Rhinoceros Bound: Cluny in the Tenth Century.* 1982

Steven D. Sargent, ed. and trans. *On the Threshold of Exact Science: Selected Writings of Anneliese Maier on Late Medieval Natural Philosophy.* 1982

Robert Somerville and Kenneth Pennington, eds. *Law, Church, and Society: Essays in Honor of Stephan Kuttner.* 1977*

Sarah Stanbury. *Seeing the* Gawain-*Poet: Description and the Act of Perception.* 1991

Susan Mosher Stuard, ed. *Women in Medieval History and Historiography.* 1987

Susan Mosher Stuard, ed. *Women in Medieval Society.* 1976

Ronald E. Surtz. *The Guitar of God: Gender, Power, and Authority in the Visionary World of Mother Juana de la Cruz (1481–1534).* 1990

Patricia Terry, trans. *Poems of the Elder Edda.* 1990

Frank Tobin. *Meister Eckhart: Thought and Language.* 1986

Ralph V. Turner. *Men Raised from the Dust: Administrative Service and Upward Mobility in Angevin England.* 1988

Harry Turtledove, trans. *The Chronicle of Theophanes: An English Translation of* anni mundi *6095–6305 (A.D. 602–813).* 1982

Mary F. Wack. *Lovesickness in the Middle Ages: The* Viaticum *and Its Commentaries.* 1990

Benedicta Ward. *Miracles and the Medieval Mind: Theory, Record, and Event, 1000–1215.* 1982

Suzanne Fonay Wemple. *Women in Frankish Society: Marriage and the Cloister, 500–900.* 1981

This book has been set in Linotron Galliard. Galliard was designed for Mergenthaler in 1978 by Matthew Carter. Galliard retains many of the features of a sixteenth century typeface cut by Robert Granjon but has some modifications that give it a more contemporary look.

Printed on acid-free paper.